A SECOND CHANCE

THE COVER: Ajāmila had been a debauchee and a criminal for most of his life. Now, at the moment of death, he saw three terrifying figures approach. They begin ripping him out of his body to take him for judgment and punishment. In great fear Ajāmila cried out to his youngest son, "Nārāyaṇa!" Suddenly four beautiful figures arrived and saved him. By the mercy of the Lord, Ajāmila had gotten a second chance.

Readers interested in the subject matter of this book are invited by the International Society for Krishna Consciousness (ISKCON) to correspond with its secretary at the following address.

International Society for Krishna Consciousness
3764 Watseka Avenue
Los Angeles, California 90034
USA

Telephone: 1-800-927-4152
http://www.harekrishna.com/~ara/
E-mail: letters@iskcon.com

First printing, 1991: 120,000
Second printing, 1995: 50,000

Printed in Portugal

Library of Congress Cataloging-in-Publication Data

A. C. Bhaktivedanta Swami Prabhupāda, 1896–1977
A second chance : the story of a near-death experience / A. C. Bhaktivedanta Swami Prabhupāda
p. cm.
Includes English translation of: Bhāgavatapurāṇa, Skandha 6, Adhyāya 1–3.
Includes index.
ISBN 0-89213-271-X
1. Purāṇas. Bhāgavatapurāṇa. Skandha 6. Adhyāya 1–3—Commentaries. I. Purāṇas. Bhāgavatapurāṇa. Skandha 6. Adhyāya 1–3. English. 1991. II. Title.
BL1140.4.B4342A2 1991
294.5'925—dc20 90—26435
CIP

A SECOND CHANCE

The Story of a Near-Death Experience

His Divine Grace
A.C. Bhaktivedanta Swami
Prabhupāda

Founder-*Ācārya* of the International Society
For Krishna Consciousness

THE BHAKTIVEDANTA BOOK TRUST

Los Angeles • London • Stockholm • Bombay • Sydney • Hong Kong

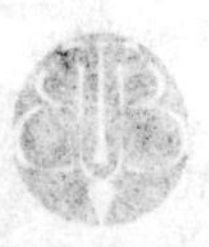

CONTENTS

Introduction

As the sinful Ajāmila lay on his deathbed, he was terrified to see three fierce humanlike creatures coming to drag him out of his dying body and take him away to the abode of Yamarāja, the lord of death, for punishment.

Surprisingly, Ajāmila escaped this terrible fate. How? You'll find out in the pages of *A Second Chance: The Story of a Near-Death Experience.*

You'll also learn many vital truths about the fundamental nature of the self and reality, so you can better prepare yourself for your own inevitable encounters with death and dying.

Even today, people momentarily on the verge of death report encounters like Ajāmila's, lending credibility to the idea that there is life after death.

In 1982, George Gallup, Jr., published a book called *Adventures in Immortality,* which contained results of a survey on American beliefs about the afterlife, including near-death and out-of-body experiences.

Sixty-seven percent of the people surveyed said they believe in life after death, and fifteen percent said they themselves had had some kind of near-death experience.

The people who reported a near-death experience were then asked to describe it. Nine percent reported an out-of-body sensation, and eight percent felt that "a special being or beings were present during the near-death experience."

The Gallup survey is intriguing, but it leaves unanswered this basic question: Is there any scientific evidence for near-death experiences, particularly of the out-of-body type?

Apparently there is—from studies of people on the verge of death who, while supposedly unconscious, accurately report events relating to their physical body from a perspective outside it. Heart attack patients, accident victims, and soldiers wounded in battle have all reported such experiences.

Dr. Michael Sabom, a cardiologist at the Emory University Medical School, undertook a scientific study of such reports. He interviewed thirty-two cardiac-arrest patients who reported out-of-body experiences. During a cardiac arrest the heart stops pumping blood to the brain, and so a patient should be totally unconscious. Yet twenty-six of the thirty-two patients reporting out-of-body experiences during cardiac arrest were able to give fairly accurate visual accounts of their resuscitation. And the remaining six gave extremely accurate accounts of the specific resuscitation techniques, matching confidential hospital records of their operations.

The results of Sabom's study, detailed in his book *Recollections of Death: A Medical Investigation* (1982), convinced him of the reality of out-of-body experiences. He concluded that the mind was an entity distinct from the brain and that the near-death crisis caused the mind and brain to split apart for a brief time. Sabom wrote, "Could the mind which splits apart from the physical brain be, in essence, the soul, which continues to exist after the final bodily death, according to some religious doctrines? As I see it, this is the ultimate question that has been raised by reports of the NDE [near-death experience]."

The true dimensions of that ultimate question are thoroughly explored in *A Second Chance,* by His Divine Grace A. C. Bhaktivedanta Swami Prabhupada, the founding spiritual master (*ācārya*) of the International Society for Krishna Consciousness.

Thousands of years ago in India, the history concerning Ajāmila and his near-death experience was related by the great spiritual master Śukadeva Gosvāmī to his disciple King Parīkṣit. Their conversation is recorded in the Sixth Canto of the Sanskrit classic *Śrīmad-Bhāgavatam,* renowned as the ripened fruit of the tree of India's timeless Vedic literature.

In 1975–76, in the course of translating the *Śrīmad-Bhāgavatam* into English, Śrīla Prabhupāda translated the story of Ajāmila. And as with the rest of the work, in addition to the text he provided an illuminating commentary on each verse.

But this wasn't the first time Śrīla Prabhupāda had explained the story of Ajāmila. During the winter of 1970–71 Śrīla Prabhupāda was traveling with some of his Western disciples in India. They had heard him speak about Ajāmila several times, and at their request he now gave a systematic series of lectures on the Ajāmila story.

Thus *A Second Chance* consists of texts from the Sixth Canto of *Śrīmad-Bhāgavatam* (reproduced here in boldface type), selections from Śrīla Prabhupāda's commentary, and excerpts from transcriptions of his lectures during the '70–71 India tour.

The history of Ajāmila is dramatic, powerful, and engaging. And the sharp philosophical and metaphysical debates that punctuate the action as Ajāmila confronts the messengers of death and finds deliverance are bound to excite the interest of those concerned with life's deepest questions.

The Publishers

1

AJĀMILA'S NEAR-DEATH EXPERIENCE

Śukadeva Gosvāmī said to King Parīkṣit: In the city known as Kānyakubja [Kanauj in present-day India] there lived a *brāhmaṇa* named Ajāmila who married a prostitute maidservant and lost all his brahminical qualities because of the association of that low-class woman. Ajāmila gave trouble to others by arresting them, by cheating them in gambling, or by directly plundering them. This was the way he earned his livelihood and maintained his wife and children. (*Śrīmad-Bhāgavatam* 6.1.21–22)

The Law of Consequences

Although Ajāmila was born of a *brāhmaṇa* father and strictly followed the regulative principles—no meat-eating, no illicit sex, no intoxication, and no gambling—he fell in love with a prostitute, and therefore all his good qualities were lost. As soon as a person abandons the regulative principles, he engages in various kinds of sinful activities. The regulative principles serve to keep us on the standard of human life. But if we abandon them, we fall down into [illegible] life [illegible].

If we want to advance in spiritual life, we must follow the regulative principles and rectify the mistakes of our past lives and this present life. Only those who have become free from all kinds of sinful reactions and are now engaged in pious activities can fully understand God. Persons who

CHAPTER 1

Separating the Men From the Animals

Śukadeva Gosvāmī said to King Parīkṣit: In the city known as Kānyakubja [Kanauj in present-day India] there lived a *brāhmaṇa* named Ajāmila who married a prostitute maid-servant and lost all his brahminical qualities because of the association of that low-class woman. Ajāmila gave trouble to others by arresting them, by cheating them in gambling, or by directly plundering them. This was the way he earned his livelihood and maintained his wife and children. (*Śrīmad-Bhāgavatam* 6.1.21–22)

The Law of Consequences

Although Ajāmila was born of a *brāhmaṇa* father and strictly followed the regulative principles—no meat-eating, no illicit sex, no intoxication, and no gambling—he fell in love with a prostitute, and therefore all his good qualities were lost. As soon as a person abandons the regulative principles, he engages in various kinds of sinful activities. The regulative principles serve to keep us on the standard of human life. But if we abandon them, we fall down into illusory life, or *māyā*.

If we want to advance in spiritual life, we must follow the regulative principles and rectify the mistakes of our past lives and this present life. Only those who have become free from all kinds of sinful reactions and are now engaged in pious activities can fully understand God. Persons who commit sinful activities and who are overly attached to bodily comforts and mundane friendship, society, and family affection cannot be spiritually self-realized.

The fault of illicit connection with women is that it destroys all one's brahminical qualities. Ajāmila abandoned all the regulative principles due to his association with a prostitute. He became a cheater and a thief. One who acts dishonestly will be punished. He may escape the king's or government's law, but he can never escape God's law. The materialists think, "I am cheating God, and I can continue to gratify my senses by all nefarious activities." But the *śāstras* (scriptures) state that such persons are cheating their own happiness in the end, because they will have to accept a material body again and suffer accordingly.

A man who is born in a *brāhmaṇa* family is expected to be truthful and self-controlled, to be fully cognizant of spiritual life and its practical application, and to have complete faith in the statements of the *śāstras.*

If a person does not follow the *śāstras,* he becomes degraded. The great sages and *ṛṣis* throughout the world have given guidance, and their words are recorded in the *śāstras.* But rascals and fools misinterpret the scriptures and misguide the people. At present, the *Bhagavad-gītā* is interpreted in so many different ways, and these so-called explanations are accepted by the innocent public as authoritative knowledge. One interpreter explains that the battlefield of Kurukṣetra refers to the material body and that the five Pāṇḍava brothers are really the five senses of the material body. But this is not the proper understanding. How can anyone explain the *Bhagavad-gītā* when he does not understand it? Such an attempt is nonsense.

To understand the bona fide science of God, one must approach a bona fide spiritual master and hear the *Bhagavad-gītā* from him. We have to follow the great personalities, the previous *ācāryas* (spiritual masters). That will be to our profit. We should not speculate and make up our own statements. We should simply accept the injunctions given by the great *ācāryas,* because that is the process of the Vedic system. One must approach a bona fide spiritual master and inquire from him submissively. The Absolute Truth is explained in the scriptures, and the scriptures are explained by the spiritual master or a saintly person. Whatever the bona fide, self-realized spiritual master says must be accepted.

There is no room for interpretation of the *śāstras.* In the *Śrīmad-Bhāgavatam* it is said that Kṛṣṇa lifted Govardhana Hill just as a child lifts a mushroom. He did it so easily, but people do not believe it. Those who do not believe in the *Bhāgavatam* interpret an indirect meaning. The meaning is clear, and there is nothing to be misunderstood, but these rascals draw their own conclusions nonetheless.

When the language is clear, why should we interpret? By interpretation, so-called scholars and theologians have played havoc with the Vedic literature. No bona fide *ācārya* has ever interpreted the *śāstras* according to his own whims, but many so-called modern scholars and leaders have done so, and therefore people are gliding down into the most abominable conditions of material existence. In the interest of the people, these rascals should be exposed. Therefore we are presenting the *Bhagavad-gītā As It Is.*

The Degradation of Modern Society

Here the *Śrīmad-Bhāgavatam* says that the *brāhmaṇa* Ajāmila became attached to a prostitute and thus lost his brahminical qualifications. He was a young man of about twenty when this happened. Because of his illicit association with the prostitute, Ajāmila was forced to live by begging, borrowing, stealing, and gambling.

These verses indicate how degraded one becomes simply by indulging in illicit sex with a prostitute. Illicit sex is not possible with chaste women, but only with unchaste women. The more society allows prostitution and illicit sex, the more impetus it gives to cheaters, thieves, plunderers, drunkards, and gamblers. Therefore we first advise all the disciples in our Kṛṣṇa consciousness movement to avoid illicit sex, which is the beginning of all abominable life and which is followed by meat-eating, gambling, and intoxication, one after another. Of course, restraint is difficult, but it is quite possible if one fully surrenders to Kṛṣṇa, since all abominable habits gradually become distasteful for a Kṛṣṇa conscious person.

While in his time Ajāmila was an exception, in the present age there are millions of Ajāmilas. But if illicit sex is allowed to increase, the entire society will be condemned, for it will be full of rogues, thieves, cheaters, and so forth.

Therefore, if we actually want to improve the world situation, we have to take to Kṛṣṇa consciousness, as that gives the best service to human society, both materially and spiritually. Whatever abominable characteristics we have developed, we have only to take to the process of *bhakti-yoga*, or devotional service, in order to completely eradicate them. We have developed so many *anarthas*, or unwanted habits, the chief of which are meat-eating, intoxication, illicit sex, and gambling. But we can curb them by accepting the principles of *bhakti-yoga* as they are presented in the *Bhagavad-gītā* and the *Śrīmad-Bhāgavatam*. Scarcely anyone knows these Vedic scriptures, and therefore no one heeds their instructions. People would rather read all kinds of books by all kinds of rascals, but the result of such books is to kill Kṛṣṇa consciousness.

In illusion a person may think he can get rid of unwanted habits and be saved by some artificial, mystic meditation. And in fact at one time it was possible to attain liberation by practicing *aṣṭāṅga-yoga*, or eightfold yogic meditation. But at present almost no one can follow this process, and artificial attempts at *yoga* will not help us.

Therefore to help the fallen people of this Age of Kali, the Supreme Lord appeared five hundred years ago as Śrī Caitanya Mahāprabhu. He knew that the people of this age would not even be able to follow the regulative principles, what to speak of practicing *aṣṭāṅga-yoga*. Therefore

He gave the *mahā-mantra*—Hare Kṛṣṇa, Hare Kṛṣṇa, Kṛṣṇa Kṛṣṇa, Hare Hare/ Hare Rāma, Hare Rāma, Rāma Rāma, Hare Hare—so that we can gradually be elevated to the highest position of spiritual life. Other processes of purification or sacrifice cannot be followed in this age, because for the most part people are too degraded. But anyone may take to this process of chanting Hare Kṛṣṇa. As it is said in the *Bṛhan-nāradīya Purāṇa* (3.8.126),

harer nāma harer nāma
harer nāmaiva kevalam
kalau nāsty eva nāsty eva
nāsty eva gatir anyathā

"In this age of quarrel and hypocrisy, the only means of deliverance is chanting the holy name of the Lord. There is no other way. There is no other way. There is no other way." Chanting the holy name of the Lord is always superbly effective, but it is especially effective in this Age of Kali. Its practical effectiveness will now be explained by Śukadeva Gosvāmī through the history of Ajāmila, who was freed from the hands of Yamarāja, the universal judge, simply because of chanting the holy name of Nārāyaṇa.

The Dangers of Illicit Sex

To benefit fully from chanting the holy name of the Lord, one needs to chant offenselessly. And to guarantee offenseless chanting, some austerity is required. First of all, one should not indulge in illicit sex. Sex is one of the bodily needs, so it is sanctioned in the *śāstras* to some degree: one is allowed to live peacefully with one's wife and have sex for begetting children. Other than to beget children, however, there is no need of indulging in sex. One who does not take the responsibility of family life but remains a bachelor and engages in illicit sex is considered irresponsible, and he will have to suffer the consequences.

Of course, one who thinks that family life is too big a

responsibility can forgo it and thus avoid a lot of trouble. Family responsibility is very great; therefore if a man feels he cannot accept the responsibility, he should remain a *brahmacārī*, a celibate student. A person who practices the science of *brahmacarya* under the care of a spiritual master automatically becomes seventy-five percent free from material entanglement.

Today, however, no one wants to undergo the austerities of *brahmacarya*. Everyone wants to remain unmarried but also engage in sex. In this way people are losing all good character. To maintain a woman who is nothing more than a prostitute and engage in illicit sex with her for producing children is sinful. Such children are unwanted (*varṇa-saṅkara*), and in this way society becomes degraded.

Ajāmila became attracted to a prostitute, and with her he begot ten children. He became so degraded that he could not execute honest business to support his large family, and he was forced to beg, borrow, and steal to maintain them. If a person indulges in illicit sex, intoxication and gambling automatically follow. His expenses will be unlimited, and to meet all his expenses he will have to adopt methods of cheating and stealing. The basis for Ajāmila's degradation was his illicit connection with the prostitute.

Therefore, in the practice of Kṛṣṇa consciousness we do not allow any illicit sex. Devotees must either get married or remain celibate; this regulation is very effective for maintaining a high standard of purity.

CHAPTER 2

In Imitation Of the Original

Śukadeva Gosvāmī continued: My dear king, eighty-eight years of his life passed by while Ajāmila thus spent his time in abominable, sinful activities to maintain his family of ten sons and the prostitute. The youngest child was a baby named Nārāyaṇa, who was naturally very dear to his father and mother. (*Śrīmad-Bhāgavatam* 6.1.23–24)

Parental Affection

Ajāmila's sinfulness is shown by the fact that although he was eighty-eight years old, he had a very young child. According to Vedic culture, one should leave home as soon as he has reached fifty years of age; one should not live at home and go on producing children. Sex is allowed for twenty-five years, between the ages of twenty-five and fifty. After that one should give up the habit of sex and leave home as a *vānaprastha* and then properly take *sannyāsa*. Ajāmila, however, because of his association with a prostitute, lost all brahminical culture and became most sinful, even in his so-called household life.

Ajāmila was a young man of twenty when he met the prostitute, and he begot ten children in her. When he was almost ninety years old, the time came when he was to die. At that time most of his children were grown up, so naturally the youngest child, Nārāyaṇa, became his parents' favorite, and Ajāmila was very much attached to him.

A baby's smile immediately attracts the father, mother, and relatives. When the child begins to talk, making sounds in broken language, it is very joyful for the parents. Unless this attraction is there, it is not possible to raise the child with affection. Parental affection is natural even among the animal species. In Kanpura, a monkey once came with her baby near the room where we were staying. The baby monkey entered the window through the bars, and the mother became very upset. She became mad with anxiety. Somehow or other we pushed the baby monkey out of the bars, and immediately the mother embraced the baby and took it away with her.

In human society, the affection between a mother and her child is very much eulogized, but as we see, this relationship is visible even among the animals. Therefore it is not an outstanding qualification; it is material nature's law. Unless the mother and child are affectionately connected, it is not possible for the child to grow up. Parental affection is natural and necessary, but it does not raise one to the spiritual platform.

The character of the debauchee Ajāmila was abominable, but he was still very affectionate toward his youngest child. Although Ajāmila was nearly ninety, he was still enjoying the child's playful pastimes, just as Mahārāja Nanda and mother Yaśodā enjoyed the childhood pastimes of Lord Kṛṣṇa.

Spiritual Affection and Variety

Parental affection in this material world is a perverted reflection of parental affection in the spiritual world, where it is found in its pure, original form. Everything originates with the transcendental reality. As stated in the *Vedānta-sūtra* (1.1.2), *janmādy asya yataḥ*: "The Supreme Absolute Truth is that from which everything emanates." If the affection between a child and his parents did not exist in the Absolute Truth, it could not exist in the material world.

Since the Absolute Truth is the source of everything, whatever varieties we see here in this material world are simply reflections of the varieties in the spiritual world. If the Absolute Truth were without variety, then where have all these varieties come from? No, the Absolute Truth is not impersonal (*nirākāra*) or without variety (*nirviśeṣa*).

Still, some persons, called Māyāvādīs, are so disappointed and frustrated with the imperfect varieties of this material world that they imagine the spiritual world to be impersonal and without variety. These impersonalists realize that they are Brahman, or spirit, but they do not know that there are innumerable planets in the *brahmajyoti*, or spiritual atmosphere. They think that the *brahmajyoti* itself is all-in-all. The impersonalists have no information of the Vaikuṇṭha planets, and due to their imperfect knowledge they again come down to these material planets. As said in the *Śrīmad-Bhāgavatam* (10.2.32):

ye 'nye 'ravindākṣa vimukta-māninas
tvayy asta-bhāvād aviśuddha-buddhayaḥ
āruhya-kṛchhrena paraṁ padaṁ tataḥ
patanty adho 'nādṛta yuṣmad aṅghrayaḥ

"Although impersonalists are almost liberated, still, on account of their negligence of the lotus feet of Kṛṣṇa, their intelligence is not yet purified. Thus despite performing severe austerities to rise up to the platform of Brahman, they must fall down again to this material world."

Spiritual Form and Spiritual Pastimes

The impersonalist philosophers cannot differentiate between activities in the material world and similar activities in the spiritual world. Nor do they differentiate between the material form and God's form. They are convinced that the impersonal *brahmajyoti,* the spiritual effulgence emanating from the Lord's body, is the Supreme Absolute Truth. The Māyāvādīs mistakenly assume that when God appears He accepts a material body, just as we have taken this material form in the material world. That kind of thinking is impersonalism, or Māyāvāda philosophy.

God has a form, but not a material form like ours. His form is *sac-cid-ānanda-vigraha,* a spiritual form full of eternity, bliss, and knowledge. Anyone who understands the transcendental nature of Kṛṣṇa's form achieves perfection. This Kṛṣṇa confirms in the *Bhagavad-gītā* (4.9):

janma karma ca me divyam
evaṁ yo vetti tattvataḥ
tyaktvā dehaṁ punar janma
naiti mām eti so 'rjuna

"When I come, I do not accept a material body; My birth and activities are completely spiritual. And anyone who perfectly understands this is liberated." When Kṛṣṇa displayed Himself as the perfect child before mother Yaśodā, He would break everything when she did not supply Him with butter—as if He were in need of butter! So God can display Himself exactly like an ordinary human being, yet He remains the Supreme Personality of Godhead.

Impersonalists cannot know God because they see Him as an ordinary man. This is rascaldom, as Kṛṣṇa declares in the *Bhagavad-gītā* (9.11): *avajānanti māṁ mūḍhāḥ.* "Only rascals accept Me as an ordinary human being." The Māyāvādīs say, "Oh, here is a child. How can He be God?" Even Brahmā and Indra became bewildered. They thought, "How can this boy be the Supreme Lord? Let me test Him."

Sometimes a so-called incarnation of God declares, "I am God." He should be tested to determine whether or not he is actually God. The Māyāvādīs are claiming, "I am God, I am Kṛṣṇa, I am Rāma." Everyone becomes "Kṛṣṇa," everyone becomes "Rāma," yet people do not challenge their claims: "If you are Rāma, exhibit your supreme potency! Rāma constructed a bridge over the Indian Ocean. What have you done? At the age of seven, Kṛṣṇa lifted Govardhana Hill. What have you done?" When they are challenged by Kṛṣṇa's pastimes, these rascals say, "It is all fiction; it is all legend." Therefore people accept an ordinary person as Rāma or Kṛṣṇa. This nonsense is going on, and both those who declare themselves to be God and those who accept them as God will have to suffer for it. Anyone can claim to be God, and any foolish person can accept, but no one will benefit by serving a false God.

Once Lord Brahmā thought that Kṛṣṇa might also be such a false God. He observed that a mere boy in Vṛndāvana, India, was accepted as the Supreme Lord and that He was performing extraordinary activities. So Brahmā decided to make a test. He took away all of Kṛṣṇa's calves and playmates and hid them. When Brahmā returned to Vṛndāvana after one year and saw the same calves and playmates still there, he could understand that Kṛṣṇa had expanded Himself by His unlimited potency into so many calves and boys. The boys' own mothers could not detect that their sons were Kṛṣṇa's expansions, though the mothers could not explain why every evening when their boys returned home from the fields, their affection for them increased more and more. Finally, Brahmā surrendered to Kṛṣṇa, composing very nice prayers in glorification of the Lord.

Similarly, Indra became bewildered when Kṛṣṇa told His father, Nanda Mahārāja, "There is no need of performing sacrifices to Indra, because he is under the order of the Supreme Lord." Kṛṣṇa did not say to Nanda Mahārāja, "I am the Supreme Lord," but He said, "Indra is under the order of the Supreme Lord; therefore he has to supply you with water. So there is no need of performing this *yajña* [sacrifice] to him."

When the sacrifice to Indra was stopped, he became furious and tried to punish the inhabitants of Vṛndāvana by sending incessant torrents of rain for seven days. Vṛndāvana was nearly drowned in water—so great was the downpour. But Kṛṣṇa, a child of about seven years, immediately lifted Govardhana Hill and invited all the residents of Vṛndāvaṇa, together with their animals, to take shelter underneath the hill. Kṛṣṇa held up the hill for seven days and nights without taking any food or rest, just to protect the residents of Vṛndāvana. Thus Indra understood that Kṛṣṇa was the Supreme Personality of Godhead.

In this way the *Śrīmad-Bhāgavatam* warns that if even great personalities like Brahmā and Indra can sometimes become bewildered by *māyā,* the external manifestation of Kṛṣṇa's energy, then what to speak of us.

So, God sometimes displays Himself as God and sometimes as a human being, but the rascal impersonalists dismiss His pastimes as legend or mythology. Either they do not believe in the *śāstras* or they interpret them in their own way, using *ardha-kukkuti-nyāya,* "the logic of half a hen." Once a man kept a hen that delivered a golden egg every day. The foolish man thought, "It is very profitable, but it is expensive to feed this hen. Better that I cut off her head and save the expense of feeding her. Then I will get the egg without any charge." The impersonalists accept the *śāstras* in this way. They think, "Oh, this is not good; it is inconvenient. We shall cut this portion out." When Kṛṣṇa says, "One should see Me everywhere," the rascal Māyāvādīs think it is very palatable, but when He says, "Give up everything and surrender to Me," they disagree. They accept what is convenient and reject what is not. But the *ācāryas* do not distort the *śāstras* in this way. When Kṛṣṇa spoke the *Bhagavad-gītā,* Arjuna said, "I accept whatever You have said."

The Absolute Truth: Full of Knowledge

The *Vedānta-sūtra* is accepted as the supreme authority of all Vedic literature. And the *Vedānta-sūtra* (1.1.2) says, *janmādy asya yataḥ:* "The Absolute Truth is the original source of everything." *Janma* means "birth." There is no question of interpretation; the meaning is clear. Everything in this material world comes out of the Absolute Truth, just as this body comes out of the womb of our mother. *Janmādy asya yataḥ:* "Beginning from birth up to the annihilation, everything is an emanation from the Absolute Truth." The Absolute Truth is that which is the source of everything, the reservoir of everything, and the maintainer of everything.

What are the characteristics of the original source? The *Śrīmad-Bhāgavatam* (1.1.1) says, *janmādy asya yato 'nvayād itarataś cārtheṣv abhijñaḥ svarāṭ:* The original source of everything must be supremely cognizant of everything, both directly and indirectly. He is the supreme spirit, and He knows everything because He is perfect. We are also spirit—spiritual sparks—and as soon as a spiritual spark takes shelter in the womb of a mother, it develops a body. That means that the spiritual spark is the source of the body and all its mechanisms. Although it is by our energy that this body is produced, we do not know how our veins are created or how our bones are created. And because we do not know, we are not God. But Kṛṣṇa knows. This is the characteristic of the Absolute Truth: He knows everything. Kṛṣṇa confirms this in the *Bhagavad-gītā* (7.26): "I know everything that has happened in the past, everything that is happening now, and everything that will happen in the future."

We become cognizant of the Absolute Truth by accepting knowledge from a spiritual master, but how has Kṛṣṇa become perfectly cognizant? How is Kṛṣṇa's knowledge so perfect? Because He is fully independent (*svarāṭ*). He does not have to learn anything from anyone. Some rascal may try to realize himself as God by taking knowledge from a Māyāvādī, but Kṛṣṇa is God without taking knowledge from anyone. That is God.

CHAPTER 3

At the Final Hour

Śukadeva Gosvāmī continued: Because of the child's broken language and awkward movements, old Ajāmila was very much attached to him. He always took care of the child and enjoyed his activities. When Ajāmila chewed food and ate it, he called the child to chew and eat, and when he drank he called the child to drink also. Always engaged in taking care of the child and calling his name, Nārāyaṇa, Ajāmila could not understand that his own time was now exhausted and that death was upon him.

When the time of death arrived for the foolish Ajāmila, he began thinking exclusively of his son Nārāyaṇa. (*Śrīmad-Bhāgavatam* 6.1.25–27)

A Child's Name

Here it is clearly mentioned that the child Nārāyaṇa was so young that he could not even speak or walk properly. Since the old man was very attached to the child, he enjoyed the child's activities, and because the child's name was Nārāyaṇa, the old man always chanted the holy name of Nārāyaṇa. Although Ajāmila was referring to the small child and not to the original Nārāyaṇa, the name of Nārāyaṇa is so powerful that even by chanting his son's name he was becoming purified. Śrīla Rūpa Gosvāmī has therefore declared that if one's mind is somehow or other attracted by the holy name of Kṛṣṇa (*tasmāt kenāpy upāyena manaḥ kṛṣṇe niveśayet*), one is on the path of liberation. In India even today parents often give their children names of God, such as Kṛṣṇa, Govinda, or Nārāyaṇa. Thus the parents chant the names Kṛṣṇa, Govinda, or Nārāyaṇa and get the chance to be purified.

At the time of death, Ajāmila was chanting the name of Nārāyaṇa in connection with his youngest child. Since Ajāmila was the son of a *brāhmaṇa,* he had been accustomed to worshiping Nārāyaṇa in his youth, because in every *brāhmaṇa's* house there is worship of Nārāyaṇa. Therefore, although the contaminated Ajāmila was calling for his son, by concentrating his mind on the holy name of Nārāyaṇa he remembered the Nārāyaṇa he had very faithfully worshiped in his youth.

The value of remembering Nārāyaṇa at the time of death is explained in the Second Canto of the *Śrīmad-Bhāgavatam* (2.1.6):

etāvān sāṅkhya-yogābhyāṁ
svadharma-pariniṣṭhayā
janma-lābhaḥ paraḥ puṁsām
ante nārāyaṇa-smṛtiḥ

"The highest perfection of human life, achieved either by complete knowledge of matter and spirit, by acquirement of mystic powers, or by perfect discharge of one's occupational duty, is to remember Nārāyaṇa, the Personality of Godhead, at the end of life."

Somehow or other, therefore, Ajāmila consciously or unconsciously chanted the name of Nārāyaṇa at the time of death and became all-perfect.

Death, a Critical Time of Life

As mentioned above, one's mentality at the time of death is all-important. But if we become complacent and think, "Oh, death takes place—what of it?" then we cannot advance on the spiritual path. Just as the air carries fragrances, so a person's mentality at the time of death will carry him to his next life. If he has cultivated the mentality of a Vaiṣṇava, a pure devotee of Kṛṣṇa, then he will immediately be transferred to Vaikuṇṭha. But if he has cultivated the mentality of an ordinary *karmī*, a fruitive worker, then he will have to stay in this material world to suffer the consequences of the kind of mentality he has thus created.

Suppose I am a businessman. If I simply do business up till the point of death, naturally my mentality will be business. One Calcutta businessman at the time of death asked about the management of his mill. He might have taken his next birth as a rat in his mill. This is possible. At the time of death, whatever you are thinking will carry you to your next body. Kṛṣṇa is very kind, and whatever mentality one is absorbed in at the time of death, Kṛṣṇa will provide an appropriate body: "All right, you are thinking like a rat? Become a rat." "You are thinking like a tiger? Become a tiger." "You are thinking like My devotee? Come to Me."

By chanting Hare Kṛṣṇa, we can mold our thoughts so that we are always thinking of Kṛṣṇa. As Kṛṣṇa recommends in the *Bhagavad-gītā* (6.47), *yoginām api sarveṣāṁ mad-gatenāntarātmanā:* "The first-class *yogī* is he who always thinks of Me within his heart." The Kṛṣṇa consciousness movement is especially meant for helping the members of human society come to this state of full Kṛṣṇa consciousness. Then at the end of life one will simply remember Kṛṣṇa. Whatever you practice throughout your life will determine your consciousness at death. That is natural.

One who properly prepares for the time of death is really intelligent, while one who thinks he can remain at home forever and enjoy the association of his wife and children is a fool. In illusion a man thinks, "My bank balance, my nice house, and my family will protect me." But these cannot protect anyone. The *Śrīmad-Bhāgavatam* (2.1.4) declares,

dehāpatya-kalatrādiṣv
ātma-sainyeṣv asatsv api
teṣāṁ pramatto nidhanaṁ
paśyann api na paśyati

"One who is mad thinks, 'My strong body, my grown-up children, my good wife, and my bank balance will save me.'" We are simply struggling in this material world like soldiers fighting on a battlefield. Our soldiers are our children, our wife, our bank balance, our countrymen, etc. The *Śrīmad-Bhāgavatam* warns us not to take shelter of such fallible soldiers. Even though a man has seen that his father and grandfather, who were once living, are existing no more, he does not see that likewise everyone, including himself, will be destroyed. How can he protect his son? How can his son protect him? These questions do not arise for the materialist who is simply engrossed in the animal propensities of eating, sleeping, defending, and mating.

CHAPTER 4

Neither Birth Nor Death

Śukadeva Gosvāmī continued: Ajāmila then saw three awkward persons with deformed bodily features, fierce, twisted faces, and hair standing erect on their bodies. With ropes in their hands, they had come to take him away to the abode of Yamarāja. When he saw them he was extremely bewildered, and because of attachment to his child, who was playing nearby, Ajāmila began to call him loudly by his name. Thus with tears in his eyes he somehow or other chanted the holy name of Nārāyaṇa. (*Śrīmad-Bhāgavatam* 6.1.28–29)

Anxious to Save Themselves from Death

At the time of death people become very anxious to save themselves, especially those who have been sinful. Of course, the soul itself is not subject to death (*na hanyate hanyamāne śarīre*), but leaving the present body and entering into another body is very painful. At death the living entity can no longer bear to remain in his present body—the pain is so acute. Sometimes when a person's life becomes too painful he commits suicide. But suicide is a sin punishable by the laws of *karma.*

When Ajāmila was dying, he saw three ferocious and very frightening persons with ropes in their hands, unruly hair on their heads, and bodily hair like bristles. These assistants of Yamarāja, the Yamadūtas, had come to drag Ajāmila out of his body and take him to the court of Yamarāja. Sometimes a dying man cries out in fear when he sees the Yamadūtas. Ajāmila, too, became very fearful.

Fortunately, even though Ajāmila was referring to his son, he chanted the holy name of Nārāyaṇa, and therefore the order-carriers of Nārāyaṇa, the Viṣṇudūtas, also immediately arrived there. Because Ajāmila was extremely afraid of the ropes of Yamarāja, he chanted the Lord's name with tearful eyes. Actually, however, he never meant to chant the holy name of Nārāyaṇa; he meant to call his son.

The Appearance and Disappearance Of Kṛṣṇa and His Devotees

One may ask, "The devotees die, and the nondevotees also die. What is the difference?" It is like this: The mother cat may catch a rat and carry it in her mouth, and she also carries her kittens in her mouth. It is the same mouth, but the kittens are comfortable and safe, whereas the rat is feeling the jaws of death. Similarly, at the time of death the devotees are transferred to the spiritual realm, Vaikuṇṭha, whereas the ordinary sinful man is dragged down to the hellish regions by the Yamadūtas, the constables of Yamarāja. This was apparently to be Ajāmila's fate.

In the *Bhagavad-gītā* (4.9) Kṛṣṇa says, *janma karma ca me divyam:* "My appearance and disappearance are spiritual, transcendental; they are not ordinary." Why does Kṛṣṇa appear in this world? That He explains in the previous verse (Bg. 4.8):

paritrāṇāya sādhūnāṁ
vināśāya ca duṣkṛtām
dharma-saṁsthāpanārthāya
sambhavāmi yuge yuge

"To deliver the pious and annihilate the miscreants, as well as to reestablish the principles of religion, I appear millennium after millennium." God's only business is to protect the faithful devotees and to kill the demoniac. Therefore we find Lord Viṣṇu pictured with His weapons, the club and *cakra* (disc), for protecting the devotees, and the lotus flower and conch for their benediction.

Similarly transcendental are the appearance and disappearance of Kṛṣṇa's devotees who are sent to this material world to preach the glories of the Lord. According to the principles of Vaiṣṇavism, both the appearance and the disappearance of such Vaiṣṇavas, or devotees of Viṣṇu (Kṛṣṇa), are all-auspicious. Therefore we hold festivals in their honor on the anniversaries of both days.

Actually, even ordinary living entities never take birth or die, what to speak of Kṛṣṇa and His devotees. Sometimes atheistic men say God is dead. They do not know that even the smallest living entity does not die. So how can God be dead? Atheists are described in the *Bhagavad-gītā* as *mūḍhās*, or foolish rascals. They have no knowledge but pose themselves as learned men and mutter something that is good neither for them nor the public.

Liberation via Thinking of Kṛṣṇa

Because somehow or other Ajāmila became absorbed in thinking of Nārāyaṇa, or Kṛṣṇa, at the time of death, he immediately became eligible for liberation, even though he had acted sinfully throughout his entire life. One can think of Kṛṣṇa in any capacity. The *gopīs*, Kṛṣṇa's cowherd girlfriends, were absorbed in thinking of Kṛṣṇa out of what appeared to be lusty desire, Śiśupāla became absorbed in thinking of Kṛṣṇa out of anger, and Kaṁsa incessantly thought of Kṛṣṇa out of fear. Kaṁsa and Śiśupāla were demons, but because they thought of the Supreme Personality of Godhead throughout their lives and at the time of death, they were granted liberation by Kṛṣṇa Himself.

Of course, it is best if one thinks of Kṛṣṇa favorably. *Bhakti*, or devotional service, means thinking favorably of Kṛṣṇa. Śiśupāla and Kaṁsa were not devotees, because the word *devotee* implies someone who is favorably disposed toward Kṛṣṇa. Thinking of Kṛṣṇa in the opposite way, however, is also accepted by Kṛṣṇa. Kṛṣṇa is so kind that anyone who thinks of Him always, even as an enemy, becomes the greatest *yogī* and attains liberation. Thus the results of yogic performances and austerities were achieved even by such inimical personalities as Kaṁsa and Śiśupāla. In the impersonal Brahman effulgence (*brahmajyoti*) we find not only the highest learned scholars (*jñānīs*), who have struggled to attain Brahman, but also those persons who constantly think of Kṛṣṇa in enmity. They also enter into that spiritual effulgence. Thus the destination achieved by the *jñānīs* is also achieved by the enemies of Kṛṣṇa. This, however, is not very desirable.

A living entity can remain for some time in the Brahman effulgence (*brahmajyoti*) as a tiny shining spiritual particle. As there are many molecular particles of sunshine, similarly the living entities can live as small particles of spiritual effulgence in the *brahmajyoti*. But they are subject to fall down into this material creation again. By nature the living entities want varieties of sense enjoyment, but in that impersonal existence there are no varieties of enjoyment. So when they desire to enjoy, they have to come again to this material world. Therefore, if one merges into the Brahman effulgence, there is every chance of falling down.

Kṛṣṇa's devotees do not desire liberation, because their only interest is to be engaged in devotional service to Kṛṣṇa, whether in the material world or in the spiritual world. Still, by the mercy of Kṛṣṇa, they attain liberation by being elevated to the planet of Goloka Vṛndāvana, the residence of Kṛṣṇa, where the material miseries of birth, death, old age, and disease are conspicuous by their absence. Thus a devotee's position is different from that of the impersonalists and *jñānīs*. The devotee's position is very exalted. He also passes through the Brahman effulgence, but he is not attracted to it. He is attracted to the Vaikuṇṭha planets, especially Goloka Vṛndāvana, where the Supreme Personality of Godhead lives eternally with His associates.

2

THE VIṢṆUDŪTAS CHALLENGE THE YAMADŪTAS

Śukadeva Gosvāmī continued: My dear king, the order-carriers of Viṣṇu, the Viṣṇudūtas, immediately arrived when they heard the holy name of their master from the mouth of the dying Ajāmila, who had certainly chanted without offense because he had chanted in complete anxiety. The order-carriers of Yamarāja were snatching the soul from the core of Ajāmila's heart, but with resounding voices the Viṣṇudūtas forbade them to do so. (*Śrīmad-Bhāgavatam* 6.1.30-31)

The Messengers Dispatched by the Lord

The Yamadūtas, who are the assistants of Yamarāja, the superintendent of death, had come to drag Ajāmila away. Ajāmila appealed to his youngest son, Nārāyaṇa: "Nārāyaṇa, please come here! I'm dying!" Kṛṣṇa is so kind that as soon as He heard Ajāmila chant "Nārāyaṇa!" at the time of his death, He immediately dispatched His assistants, the Viṣṇudūtas, to give Ajāmila shelter.

Śrīla Viśvanātha Cakravartī Ṭhākura remarks that the Viṣṇudūtas came because they heard Ajāmila chant the holy name of their master, Nārāyaṇa, without considering why he was chanting. While chanting the name of Nārāyaṇa, Ajāmila was actually thinking of his son, but simply because they heard Ajāmila chant the Lord's name, the Viṣṇudūtas immediately came for Ajāmila's protection.

CHAPTER 5

The Viṣṇudūtas To the Rescue

Śukadeva Gosvāmī continued: My dear king, the order-carriers of Viṣṇu, the Viṣṇudūtas, immediately arrived when they heard the holy name of their master from the mouth of the dying Ajāmila, who had certainly chanted without offense because he had chanted in complete anxiety. The order-carriers of Yamarāja were snatching the soul from the core of Ajāmila's heart, but with resounding voices the Viṣṇudūtas forbade them to do so. (*Śrīmad-Bhāgavatam* 6.1.30–31)

The Messengers Dispatched by the Lord

The Yamadūtas, who are the assistants of Yamarāja, the superintendent of death, had come to drag Ajāmila away. Ajāmila appealed to his youngest son, Nārāyaṇa: "Nārāyaṇa, please come here! I'm dying!" Kṛṣṇa is so kind that as soon as He heard Ajāmila chant "Nārāyaṇa!" at the time of his death, He immediately dispatched His assistants, the Viṣṇudūtas, to give Ajāmila shelter.

Śrīla Viśvanātha Cakravartī Ṭhākura remarks that the Viṣṇudūtas came because they heard Ajāmila chant the holy name of their master, Nārāyaṇa, without considering why he was chanting. While chanting the name of Nārāyaṇa, Ajāmila was actually thinking of his son, but simply because they heard Ajāmila chant the Lord's name, the Viṣṇudūtas immediately came for Ajāmila's protection.

Chanting of the Lord's holy name is actually meant for His glorification. Ajāmila, however, did not glorify the Lord: he simply chanted the holy name of Nārāyaṇa because of his excessive attachment to his son. Nevertheless, because of his past good fortune in having rendered devotional service to Nārāyaṇa in his youth, he apparently chanted the holy name in full devotional service and without offense. Thus that chanting was sufficient to cleanse him of all sinful reactions and assure him the protection of the Viṣṇudūtas.

The name Nārāyaṇa has the full potency of the Supreme Personality of Godhead—Nārāyaṇa, or Kṛṣṇa. That is the secret of *nāma-saṅkīrtana,* chanting the names of God. By chanting the holy name of Kṛṣṇa, we make immediate contact with Kṛṣṇa Himself. The reason for this is that the Lord's name is not material: it is spiritual and absolute. Thus there is no difference between Kṛṣṇa and His name.

Snatching the Soul

When the Viṣṇudūtas arrived, they spoke to the Yamadūtas with extreme gravity: "What are you doing? Stop! You cannot take this man to Yamarāja!"

A Vaiṣṇava, one who has surrendered to the lotus feet of Lord Viṣṇu, is always protected by Lord Viṣṇu's order-carriers. Because Ajāmila had chanted the holy name of Nārāyaṇa, the Viṣṇudūtas not only immediately arrived on the spot but also at once ordered the Yamadūtas not to touch him. By speaking with resounding voices, the Viṣṇudūtas threatened to punish the Yamadūtas if they continued trying to snatch Ajāmila's soul from his heart. The order-carriers of Yamarāja have jurisdiction over all sinful living entities, but the messengers of Lord Viṣṇu are capable of punishing anyone, including Yamarāja, if he wrongs a Vaiṣṇava.

Modern scientists do not know where to find the soul within the body with their material instruments, but here the *Śrīmad-Bhāgavatam* clearly explains that the soul is within the core of the heart (*hṛdaya*); it is from the heart that the Yamadūtas were trying to extract the soul of Ajāmila. The heart is part of the mechanical arrangement of the body. As the Lord says in the *Bhagavad-gītā* (18.61):

īśvaraḥ sarva-bhūtānāṁ
hṛd-deśe 'rjuna tiṣṭhati
bhrāmayan sarva-bhūtāni
yantrārūḍhāni māyayā

"The Supreme Lord is situated in everyone's heart, O Arjuna, and is directing the wanderings of all living entities, who are seated as on a machine made of the material energy." *Yantra* means "machine," such as an automobile. The driver of the machine of the body is the individual soul, who is also its director or proprietor, but the supreme director and proprietor is the Personality of Godhead in His form as the Supersoul.

One's body is created through the agency of *māyā* according to one's activities in one's past life; and according to one's activities in this life, *māyā* creates another body for the next life. At the appropriate time, one's next body is immediately chosen, and both the individual soul and the Supersoul transfer to that particular bodily machine. This is the process of transmigration of the soul.

During transmigration from one body to the next, the sinful soul is taken away by the order-carriers of Yamarāja and put into a particular type of hellish life in order to become accustomed to the condition in which he will live in his next body.

CHAPTER 6

The Residents Of the Spiritual Sky

Śukadeva Gosvāmī continued: When the order-carriers of Yamarāja, the son of the sun-god, were thus forbidden, they replied, "Who are you, sirs, that have the audacity to challenge the jurisdiction of Yamarāja? Whose servants are you, where have you come from, and why are you forbidding us to touch the body of Ajamila? Are you demigods from the heavenly planets, are you sub-demigods, or are you the best of devotees? Your eyes are just like the petals of lotus flowers. Dressed in yellow silken garments, decorated with garlands of lotuses, and wearing very attractive helmets on your heads and earrings on your ears, you all appear fresh and youthful. Your four long arms are decorated with bows and quivers of arrows and with swords, clubs, conchshells, discs, and lotus flowers. Your effulgence has dissipated the darkness here with extraordinary illumination. Now, sirs, why are you obstructing us?" (*Śrīmad-Bhāgavatam* 6.1.32–36)

Divine Interference

The sins Ajāmila had committed placed him within the jurisdiction of Yamarāja, the supreme judge appointed to consider the sins of the living entities. When forbidden to touch Ajāmila, the order-carriers of Yamarāja were surprised, because within all the three worlds no one had ever before hindered them in the execution of their duty.

The Viṣṇudūtas were coming from Vaikuṇṭha, and they appeared extraordinary, each with four arms. The servants of Yamarāja immediately received them with respect. They had no idea which planet the Viṣṇudūtas had come from, so they simply suggested, "You must have come from a very exalted planet, but why are you interfering with our business? We are Yamadūtas. It is our duty to arrest every sinful man, and Ajāmila has committed misdeeds throughout his life. Now, at the end of his life, we are authorized to take him to Yamarāja, the son of Vivasvān, the sun-god, so why are you preventing us?"

The most significant word used in verse 32 is *siddha-sattamāḥ,* which means "the best of the perfect." In the *Bhagavad-gītā* (7.3) it is said, *manuṣyāṇāṁ sahasreṣu kaścid yatati siddhaye:* out of millions of persons, one may try to become *siddha,* perfect—or, in other words, self-realized. A self-realized person knows that he is not the body but a spiritual soul (*ahaṁ brahmāsmi*). At present almost no one is aware of this fact, but one who understands this has attained perfection and is therefore called *siddha.* When one understands that the soul is part and parcel of the Supreme Soul and one thus engages in the devotional service of the Supreme Soul, one becomes *siddha-sattama.* One is then eligible to live in Vaikuṇṭha or Kṛṣṇaloka. The word *siddha-sattama,* therefore, refers to a pure devotee of the Lord.

Since the Yamadūtas are servants of Yamarāja, who is also one of the *siddha-sattamas,* they knew that a *siddha-sattama* is above the demigods and sub-demigods and, indeed, above all the living entities within this material world. The Yamadūtas therefore inquired why the Viṣṇudūtas were preventing them from carrying out the orders of such an exalted soul as Yamarāja.

It should also be noted that Ajāmila was not yet dead, for the Yamadūtas had been stopped before they could snatch the soul from his heart. Ajāmila was simply on the verge of death as the argument progressed between the Yamadūtas and the Viṣṇudūtas. The conclusion of that argument was to be a decision regarding who would claim the soul of Ajāmila.

Spiritual Beauty

The Viṣṇudūtas exactly resembled Lord Viṣṇu. The Yamadūtas had never seen them before, because the Yamadūtas stay in an atmosphere where only sinful activities are executed. Therefore they were astonished at the presence of these beautiful personalities and said, "By your bodily features you appear to be very exalted gentlemen, and you have such celestial power that you have dissipated the darkness of this material world with your effulgence. Why then should you endeavor to stop us from executing our duty?" It will be explained that the Yamadūtas, the order-carriers of Yamarāja, mistakenly considered Ajāmila sinful. They did not know that although he was sinful throughout his entire life, he was purified by constantly chanting the holy name of Nārāyaṇa.

The Viṣṇudūtas were so effulgent because they were residents of the spiritual world, where everyone and every thing is self-effulgent. As Lord Kṛṣṇa says in the *Bhagavad-gītā* (15.6), *na tad bhāsayate sūryo na śaśāṅko na pāvakaḥ:* "My abode is not illuminated by the sun, the moon, fire, or electricity." The Yamadūtas did not know where the Viṣṇudūtas had come from, but they could see that the Viṣṇudūtas were not ordinary, since they were so effulgent, they had four arms, and they were extremely beautiful.

The dress and bodily features of the residents of Vaikuṇṭha are accurately described in these verses. The residents of Vaikuṇṭha, who are decorated with garlands and yellow silken garments, have four arms holding a disc, flower, club, and conchshell. Thus they exactly resemble Lord Viṣṇu—except for one very prominent feature: the Kaustubha jewel, which the Lord wears on His chest. The residents of Vaikuṇṭha have the same bodily features as Nārāyaṇa because they have attained the liberation of *sārūpya,* but they nevertheless act as servants. All the residents of Vaikuṇṭhaloka know perfectly well that their master is Nārāyaṇa, or Kṛṣṇa, and that they are all His servants. They are all self-realized souls who are *nitya-mukta,* everlastingly liberated. Although they could conceivably declare themselves Nārāyaṇa, they never do so; they always remain Kṛṣṇa conscious and serve the Lord faithfully. Such is the atmosphere of Vaikuṇṭhaloka. Similarly, one who learns the faithful service of Lord Kṛṣṇa through the Kṛṣṇa consciousness movement will always remain in Vaikuṇṭhaloka and have nothing to do with the material world.

Beyond the Material World

In our conditioned state, we cannot know about the spiritual world. But the spiritual world exists. As Lord Kṛṣṇa states in the *Bhagavad-gītā* (8.20), *paras tasmāt tu bhāvo 'nyo:* "Besides this inferior, material nature there is another, superior nature." This material nature is one nature, comprised of millions and trillions of universes clustered together in one corner of the spiritual sky. We cannot even measure the sky covered by this one universe, within which there are innumerable planets; yet there are millions and trillions of universes in the entire material creation. And the entire material creation is only one fourth of existence. In other words, this whole material world is existing in one fourth of Kṛṣṇa's energy. The other three fourths comprise the spiritual sky. Unfortunate persons think that this planet is all in all, but this is frog philosophy. A frog in a well cannot understand anything beyond the well, and he measures everything in terms of his well. When he is told about the ocean, he cannot imagine it. Similarly, persons with such a frog's mentality imagine, "God is like this," or "God's kingdom is like that," or "I am God," or "There is no God." But this is all foolishness.

CHAPTER 7

Authorized Discrimination

Śukadeva Gosvāmī continued: Being thus addressed by the messengers of Yamarāja, the servants of Vāsudeva smiled and spoke the following words in voices as deep as the sound of rumbling clouds: "If you are actually servants of Yamarāja, you must explain to us the meaning of religious principles and the symptoms of irreligion. What is the process of punishing others? Who are the actual candidates for punishment? Are all persons engaged in fruitive activities punishable, or only some of them?" (*Śrīmad-Bhāgavatam* 6.1.37–39)

What the Representatives of Dharma Should Know

The Yamadūtas protested to the Viṣṇudūtas, "You are so exalted that it is not very good for you to interfere with our business." The Yamadūtas were surprised to see that the Viṣṇudūtas, although exalted souls, were hindering the rule of Yamarāja. Similarly, the Viṣṇudūtas were also surprised that the Yamadūtas, although claiming to be servants of Yamarāja, the supreme judge of religious principles, were unaware of the principles of religion. Thus the Viṣṇudūtas smiled, thinking, "What is this nonsense they are speaking? If they are actually servants of Yamarāja, they should know that Ajāmila is not a suitable candidate for them to carry off."

The Viṣṇudūtas began to speak in grave voices: "You claim to be the representatives of Dharmarāja [Yamarāja], the superintendent of death and the maintainer of religion, and you accuse us of interfering in your business, which he has entrusted to you. Therefore would you kindly explain what is *dharma*, or religion, and what is *adharma*, or irreligion? If you are actually representatives of Yamaraja, then you can answer this question."

This inquiry put by the Viṣṇudūtas to the Yamadūtas is most important. A servant must know the instructions of his master. The servants of Yamarāja claimed to be carrying out his orders, and therefore the Viṣṇudūtas very intelligently asked them to explain religious and irreligious principles. A Vaiṣṇava knows these principles perfectly well because he is well acquainted with the instructions of the Supreme Personality of Godhead. The Supreme Lord says, *sarva-dharmān parityajya mām ekaṁ śaraṇaṁ vraja:* "Give up all varieties of religion and just surrender unto Me." Therefore surrender unto the Supreme Personality of Godhead is the actual principle of religion. Those who have surrendered to the demands of material nature instead of to Kṛṣṇa are all impious, regardless of their material position. Unaware of the principles of religion, they do not surrender to Kṛṣṇa, and therefore they are considered sinful rascals, the lowest of men, and fools bereft of all knowledge. As Kṛṣṇa says in the *Bhagavad-gītā* (7.15):

na māṁ duṣkṛtino mūḍhāḥ
prapadyante narādhamāḥ
māyayāpahṛta-jñānā
āsuraṁ bhāvam āśritāḥ

"Those miscreants who are grossly foolish, who are the lowest among mankind, whose knowledge is stolen by illusion, and who partake of the atheistic nature of demons do not surrender unto Me."

The question posed by the Viṣṇudūtas was very suitable. One who represents someone else must fully know that person's mission. The devotees in the Kṛṣṇa consciousness movement must therefore be fully aware of the mission of

Kṛṣṇa and Lord Caitanya and the philosophy of Kṛṣṇa consciousness; otherwise they will be considered foolish.

Lord Caitanya Mahāprabhu has said, *yei kṛṣṇa-tattva-vettā, sei 'guru' haya*: "One must know Kṛṣṇa—then he can become a *guru*." Not just anyone can become a *guru*. Thus the Viṣṇudūtas challenged the Yamadūtas: "If you are truly representatives of Dharmarāja, then you must explain what is religion and what is irreligion." That should be the criterion for determining who is actually representative of religion. It is not that everyone should be accepted as religious or as a *guru*. Widespread ignorance has given rise to many persons calling themselves God, representing so much nonsense in the name of *dharma*. When someone says, "I am God," or "I have become God by mystic *yoga*," one should challenge him. In America a man claimed, "I am God, everyone is God," and thus gathered disciples. One day he was suffering from a toothache, and I asked him, "What kind of God are you that you are suffering so much from a toothache?" Only a lunatic or a cheater claims, "I am God."

Officers of Law Enforcement

One who has the power to punish others should not punish everyone. There are innumerable living entities, most of whom are in the spiritual world and are *nitya-mukta*, everlastingly liberated. There is no question of judging these liberated living beings. Only a small fraction of the living entities, perhaps one fourth, are in the material world. And the major portion of the living entities in the material world—8,000,000 of the 8,400,000 forms of life—are lower than human beings. They are not punishable, for under the laws of material nature they are automatically evolving. Human beings, who are advanced in consciousness, are responsible for their actions, but not all humans are punishable. Those engaged in advanced pious activities are beyond punishment. Only those who engage in sinful activities are punishable. Therefore the Viṣṇudūtas particularly inquired about the criteria Yamarāja uses to determine who is punishable and who is not. How is one to be judged? What is the basic principle of authority? These are the questions raised by the Viṣṇudūtas.

The Yamadūtas felt that they were faultless because they were following the orders of Yamarāja, who himself is faultless. Just because a magistrate has to direct the punishment of those who transgress the law does not mean the magistrate is a criminal. He is a representative of the government. Similarly, although Yamarāja has jurisdiction over the regions of hell and deals with all sinful persons, he is a pure representative of Kṛṣṇa and simply executes the order of his master.

A police constable is supposed to know the law and whom to arrest for breaking the law. If he arrests anyone and everyone, then he himself is a criminal. He may not arrest the law-abiding citizens. Similarly, the Yamadūtas cannot take away just anyone and everyone to the court of Yamarāja. They can take only the nondevotees to be punished for their sinful acts. Yamarāja has especially cautioned the Yamadūtas not to approach Vaiṣṇavas.

However, because Ajāmila had been very sinful, the Yamadūtas could not understand why he should not be considered a criminal and be brought to Yamarāja for punishment.

Devotees and Demons

There are two classes of people in this material world: those who are servants of God, called *devas* or *suras,* and those who are servants of *māyā* (illusion), called *asuras.*

In the spiritual world, however, there is only one class, because the inhabitants are all servants of God. Therefore the spiritual world is called absolute. There is no disagreement in the spiritual world, as the center is Kṛṣṇa, or God, and everyone there is engaged in His service out of love, not as a paid servant. A paid servant will serve in proportion to the money he receives, but in Vaikuṇṭha there is no question of being a paid servant. Everyone is liberated, and everyone is as opulent as the Supreme Personality of Godhead, but everyone is still a servant. In the material world people serve out of need, but in the spiritual world everyone serves out of love. There is no need for anything, because everything there is complete. The *Brahma-saṁhitā* says that in the spiritual world there are *kalpa-vṛkṣa,* or desire trees, from which one can get anything he desires.

In the material world, service is forced upon everyone. If someone does not render service, he will starve. Even a king has to work, what to speak of the poor man. Under the direction of the Supreme Lord, the material energy makes everyone into a dancing dog. The master says, "Please dance," and the dog dances, because he knows that unless he performs, he will starve.

Whether in the material world or the spiritual world, everyone is a servant, but here people are under the impression that they are masters. The head of the family thinks, "I am the master of my wife and children." But in fact he is serving each and every member of his family. The state executive officer thinks, "I am the king" or "I am the president," but actually he is the servant of the citizens. Servitude is his position, and unless he serves the citizens according to their expectations, he will be deposed or fail to win reelection.

In the material world everyone is trying to become master of all he surveys, and thus there is competition on every level—between self-acclaimed "Gods," between heads of state, even between friends and family members. In this illusory competition to be master, everyone fails. Mahātmā Gandhi was respected as the father of India, but after all he was just a servant, and when one man didn't like his service, Gandhi was killed. Similarly, President Kennedy was a very popular president, but somebody saw some discrepancy in his service, and he was also killed. No one is really the master here. Everyone is either a servant of *māyā* (illusion) or a servant of God.

Everyone has to obey the government laws. Under the spell of illusion, however, the criminal thinks, "I do not accept the government laws." Yet when he is caught he is forced to obey the government laws in the prison house. He has no choice. Similarly, we are all servants of God, but the demoniac class of men (*asuras*) do not care about God and God's laws. These rascals think that there is no God, or that everyone is God, or that they themselves are God. But such "Gods" must also follow the laws of God in the form of birth, death, disease, and old age.

Only persons who are totally illusioned refuse to serve God. Instead of voluntarily rendering service to God, they are the slaves of *māyā*, the illusory energy of God. A person who is haunted by ghosts speaks all kinds of nonsense. Similarly, when a living entity is haunted by *māyā*, or engrossed by the illusory effects of the material nature, he also talks foolish nonsense, and the most foolish talk is to claim that he is God.

Among the two classes of men—the divine (*devas*) and the demoniac (*asuras*)—there is an ongoing struggle. The *asuras* are always rebelling against God, and the *devas* are always surrendering to God. In the story of Prahlāda Mahārāja, we see that even among family members there are *devas* and *asuras*. Prahlāda Mahārāja's father, Hiraṇyakaśipu, was an *asura*, whereas Prahlāda Mahārāja was a *deva*. Naturally a father is affectionate toward his child, but because Hiraṇyakaśipu was a demon, he became the enemy of his son. That is the nature of demons.

Of course, even a tiger has affection for her cubs, and so at first Hiraṇyakaśipu showed affection for Prahlāda Mahārāja, who was a very well mannered and attractive child at five years old. One day Hiraṇyakaśipu asked his son, "My dear boy, what is the best thing you have learned in school? Tell me."

Prahlāda Mahārāja replied, "One should sacrifice everything to realize God. This human form of life is the best opportunity we have for making spiritual progress, and it must be utilized for realizing God."

Hiraṇyakaśipu angrily inquired from his son's teachers, "Why have you taught all this nonsense to my boy?"

They fearfully answered, "Sir, we did not teach these things to this boy. He is naturally inclined toward God, so what can we do? As soon as he gets the opportunity, he begins to teach God consciousness to the other boys in the class." In the absence of his teachers, Prahlāda Mahārāja would immediately stand up on the bench and address his friends, "My dear boys, this life is not for enjoying sense gratification. It is for realizing God. Do not forget this."

Similarly, we have taken up this preaching mission because people in general are interested only in immediate sense gratification, which is not good for them. In the *Śrīmad-Bhāgavatam* (5.5.4) Lord Ṛṣabhadeva says, *nūnaṁ pramattaḥ kurute vikarma yad indriya-prītaya āpṛnoti:* "Simply for sense gratification people are committing so many sinful activities. They are just like madmen." A madman does not know what he is doing. Materialistic persons are so much engrossed in their pursuit of sense gratification that they have become maddened and commit all kinds of sins.

Lord Ṛṣabhadeva says that the materialistic way of life is very risky. For those who indulge in sense gratification, Kṛṣṇa gives the facility, forcing them to take birth again in the material atmosphere. A monkey has very good facility for enjoying sex. In some ways a monkey is renounced: he lives naked in the forest, he eats only fruit. But his nature is that he must have at least three dozen wives for sex enjoyment. So-called renunciants who wear the cloth of a *sādhu* but secretly enjoy illicit sex with women are just like monkeys. This is demoniac.

Demons, or *asuras*, do not believe in God and act according to their own whims. In the *Bhagavad-gītā* (7.15), Kṛṣṇa describes them as follows:

na māṁ duṣkṛtino mūḍhāḥ
prapadyante narādhamāḥ

māyayāpahṛta-jñānā
āsuraṁ bhāvam āśritāḥ

"Those miscreants who are grossly foolish, who are lowest among mankind, whose knowledge is stolen by illusion, and who partake of the atheistic nature of demons do not surrender unto Me." Here Kṛṣṇa clearly states, *āsuraṁ bhāvam āśritāḥ:* because the demons have taken shelter of atheistic philosophy, they are the lowest of mankind despite their advancement of education, science, and politics. Someone might object, "How can you call an atheistic gentleman with a university degree a demon? He is so educated and highly qualified." The verdict of the *śāstra* is that although he appears to be very learned, his actual knowledge has been stolen away by *māyā* on account of his being atheistic.

Scriptural injunctions may not be very palatable; nonetheless, they are authoritative, and we have to preach the truth. We cannot play hide and seek with the problems of life. We must know our real position, and we must know what is religion and what is irreligion. Religion means action according to the orders of God, and irreligion means action that goes against the orders of God.

CHAPTER 8

Religion

The Yamadūtas replied, "That which is prescribed in the *Vedas* constitutes *dharma*, and the opposite of that is irreligion. The *Vedas* are directly the Supreme Personality of Godhead, Nārāyaṇa, and are self-born. This we have heard from Yamarāja." (*Śrīmad-Bhāgavatam* 6.1.40)

Hearing from Authority

Vedic principles are accepted as authoritative because they originate with Kṛṣṇa. Thus the *Vedas* carry the authority of the Supreme Personality of Godhead in the same way that lawbooks carry the authority of the government.

When it comes to determining what is religion and what is irreligion, there is no such thing as "This is my opinion" or "I think it means this." Opinion is nonsense. We have to understand God by the process of *śuśruma*, hearing from the authorized representative of God. In the *Bhagavad-gītā* (4.1) Kṛṣṇa says,

imaṁ vivasvate yogaṁ
proktavān aham avyayam
vivasvān manave prāha
manur ikṣvākave bravīt

"I instructed this imperishable science of *yoga* to the sun-god, Vivasvān, and Vivasvān instructed it to Manu, the father of mankind, and Manu in turn instructed it to Ikṣvāku." This is the way to understand the *Vedas:* by hearing from the proper authority, the spiritual master.

So the Yamadūtas were claiming that the Viṣṇudūtas should not hinder them in the performance of their duty since they were acting under the order of a bona fide authority, Yamarāja. Yamarāja is one of the twelve *mahājanas,* great personalities who are authorities in both spiritual and material affairs. He is a Vaiṣṇava, but his thankless task is to punish all the souls who perform sinful activities. Just as the superintendent of police is a responsible, faithful servant of the government, so Yamarāja is a faithful servant of Lord Nārāyaṇa, or Kṛṣṇa. His task is to chastise sinful persons. If a high-court judge is required in ordinary government, why not in God's government?

There are twelve *mahājanas* mentioned in the *Śrīmad-Bhāgavatam:* Lord Brahmā; Nārada Muni; Lord Śiva; the four Kumāras; Lord Kapila, the son of Devahūti; Svayambhuva Manu; Prahlāda Mahārāja; Bhīṣmadeva; Janaka Mahārāja; Śukadeva Gosvāmī; Bali Mahārāja; and Yamarāja. These authorities know exactly who God is, and they can direct us to Him. Therefore the *śāstras* advise us to follow them.

Without following the *mahājanas,* it is impossible to know God, because we cannot understand the path of religion by our mental speculation. Religious principles are enunciated by the Supreme Personality of Godhead (*dharmaṁ tu sākṣād bhagavat-praṇītam*). Therefore real religion means to abide by the words of the Supreme Lord and His representatives. In the *Bhagavad-gītā* (18.66) Kṛṣṇa says, *māṁ ekaṁ śaraṇaṁ vraja:* "Simply surrender unto Me." That is true religion. Anything else is irreligion. Manmade religion is not religion; it is cheating. Nowadays it has become fashionable for everyone to manufacture his own religion without reference to the authorities. One should know that *dharma,* or religion, means the laws given to man by God. The path of *dharma* is strictly followed by the *mahājanas,* and so we have to follow them. Otherwise there is no possibility of understanding what religion is or who God is.

Everyone in the material world is puzzled about what religion is. Therefore, the *Mundaka Upaniṣad* (1.2.12) says, one should approach a *guru: tad vijñānārthaṁ sa gurum evābhigacchet.* "If someone wants to learn the transcendental science, he has to approach a *guru.*" There are no exceptions. One cannot say, "I shall learn the transcendental science without going to a spiritual master." No. That is not possible. The Vaiṣṇava principles enjoin, *ādau gurv-āśrayam:* the first step in understanding spiritual knowledge is to take shelter of a bona fide *guru.* And there are three principles to observe in taking shelter of a *guru: tad viddhi praṇipātena paripraśnena sevayā.* We must surrender to the spiritual master, we must inquire from him, and we must render service to him. Then we will be able to understand real spiritual knowledge.

When Sanātana Gosvāmī approached Lord Caitanya to become His disciple, Sanātana surrendered himself and said, "My dear Lord, when I was a minister, people used to address me as a learned man, and so I accepted that I was learned and intelligent. But actually I am neither learned nor intelligent, because I do not know what I am. This is the result of my learning: I know everything except what I am and how to get out of this miserable material condition of life."

We see that modern education fails here also. The professor talks about so many things, but if we ask him what he is, he has no answer. Universities award degrees to the graduates, who think, "I am a Ph.D., a very learned man," but if we ask that Ph.D. to explain what he is and what the purpose of life is, he will refer only to his bodily designations: "I am American, I am male, etc." He can only state his identification with the body, which he is not, and therefore he is fool number one.

At first Arjuna was also thinking in terms of bodily connections: "Kṛṣṇa, how can I fight? On the other side there are my cousins, my brothers, my uncles, my nephews, and my brothers-in-law. If I kill them, their wives will become widows and be polluted, and there will be unwanted children." Arjuna was a very learned man, but he was perplexed. He said, "My dear Kṛṣṇa, now I am puzzled. I am a *kṣatriya*, and it is my duty to fight, but I am deviating from this duty because I am bewildered and cannot reason clearly. I know You can explain to me what I should do; therefore I surrender unto You as Your disciple. Please instruct me." (*Bhagavad-gītā* 2.7)

The Vedic literature advises us first of all that the *guru* is not a plaything. One should not think, "I must have a *guru* because it is fashionable, but there is no need to obey his order." That kind of *guru* is useless, and that kind of disciple is useless also. Accepting a *guru* is very serious. You must seriously find out who is a bona fide spiritual master, one who can solve the problems of your life. Only when one is serious about getting out of the blazing fire of material existence should one approach a spiritual master.

The *Śrīmad-Bhāgavatam* (11.3.21) says,

tasmād guruṁ prapadyeta
jijñāsuḥ śreya uttamam
śabde pare ca niṣṇātaṁ
brahmaṇy upaśamāśrayam

One who wants the ultimate benefit in his life must surrender to a *guru*. The *guru* must be well versed in the Vedic literature and know its conclusions. And not only must he be well versed in the scripture, but in his life he must have adopted the path of Vedic principles, without deviating in any way. He must be finished with all hankerings for wealth, women, and prestige, and he must be fully situated in spiritual life, completely surrendered to the Supreme Personality of Godhead, Kṛṣṇa. One should try to find such a personality and accept him as one's spiritual master.

So the servants of Yamarāja replied quite properly. They did not manufacture principles of religion or irreligion.

Instead, they explained what they had heard from their spiritual master, Yamarāja. *Mahājano yena gataḥ sa panthāḥ:* one should follow the *mahājana*, the authorized person. Yamarāja is one of twelve authorities. Therefore the servants of Yamarāja, the Yamadūtas, replied with perfect justification when they said *śuśruma:* "We have heard from our master, Yamarāja."

CHAPTER 9

Punishment

The Yamadūtas continued, "The supreme cause of all causes, Nārāyaṇa, is situated in His abode in the spiritual world, but still He controls the entire cosmic manifestation according to the modes of material nature—goodness, passion, and ignorance. In this way all living entities are awarded different qualities, different names (such as *brāhmaṇa, kṣatriya,* and *vaiśya*), different duties according to the *varṇāśrama* institution, and different forms. Thus Nārāyaṇa is the cause of the entire cosmic manifestation.

"The sun, fire, sky, air, demigods, moon, evening, day, night, directions, water, land, and the Supersoul Himself all witness the activities of the living entity. The candidates for punishment are those who are confirmed by these many witnesses to have deviated from their prescribed duties. Everyone engaged in fruitive activities is suitable to be subjected to punishment according to his sinful acts.

"O inhabitants of Vaikuṇṭha, you are sinless, but those within this material world are all fruitive workers, whether acting piously or impiously. Both kinds of action are possible for them because they are contaminated by the three modes of nature and must act accordingly. One who has accepted a material body cannot be inactive, and sinful action is inevitable for one acting under the modes of material nature. Therefore all the living entities within this material world are punishable. Thus in proportion to the extent of one's religious or irreligious actions in this life, one must enjoy or suffer the corresponding reactions of his *karma* in the next." (*Śrīmad-Bhāgavatam* 6.1.41–45)

The Cause Behind All Activities

The *Śvetāśvatara Upaniṣad* (6.8) informs us,

na tasya kāryaṁ karaṇaṁ ca vidyate
na tat-samaś cābhyadhikaś ca dṛśyate
parāsya śaktir vividhaiva śrūyate
svābhāvikī jñāna-bala-kriyā ca

Nārāyaṇa, the Supreme Personality of Godhead, is almighty, omnipotent. He has multifarious energies, and therefore He is able to remain in His own abode and without endeavor supervise and manipulate the entire cosmic manifestation through the interaction of the three modes of material nature—goodness, passion, and ignorance. These interactions create different forms, bodies, activities, and changes, which all occur perfectly. Because the Lord is perfect, everything works as if He were directly supervising and taking part in it.

Atheistic men, however, being covered by the three modes of material nature, cannot see that Nārāyaṇa is the supreme cause behind all activities. Lord Kṛṣṇa confirms this in the *Bhagavad-gītā* (7.13),

tribhir guṇa-mayair bhāvair
ebhiḥ sarvam idaṁ jagat
mohitaṁ nābhijānāti
mām ebhyaḥ param avyayam

"Deluded by the three modes, the whole world does not know Me, who am above the modes and inexhaustible."

Compelled to Work

There are three energies of the Supreme Lord: the internal energy (*parā-śakti*), the marginal energy, and the external energy. The living entities belong to the marginal energy because they can come under the influence of either the internal or external energy of the Lord. By nature they also belong to the *parā-śakti*, but when they come under the control of the material energy they are known as *kṣetra-jña-śakti*, "knowers of the material field." In other words, the direct, internal energy of God is spiritual (*parā*), and the living entities have this same nature (*parā*), but in contact with the material energy (*kṣetra*), the living entity accepts a material body as his self and is thus forced to act, manipulating the five senses.

The Yamadūtas say that everyone with a material body must work. An ant and an elephant both have to work. The ant requires only a grain of sugar for his sustenance, whereas the elephant requires three hundred kilograms of food daily, but both must work for it. Foolish people say that the Vaiṣṇavas do not work, but the Vaiṣṇavas work for Kṛṣṇa twenty-four hours a day. They are not idle do-nothings. While we are in this material world, we have to work, but we work for Kṛṣṇa. That is not really work, or *karma:* it is *dharma*, practical religion. Unless one works for Kṛṣṇa, all his labor is *adharma*, irreligious sense gratification.

On the Basis of a Man's Nature

The real aim of life is to satisfy Kṛṣṇa, and *varṇāśrama-dharma* is the institution of that ideal in human society. The *varṇāśrama* system divides society into four spiritual orders (*āśramas*) and four social classes (*varṇas*). The spiritual orders are the *brahmacārīs* (celibate students), the *gṛhasthas* (householders living under spiritual regulation), the *vānaprasthas* (retirees), and the *sannyāsīs* (renunciants). The four social orders are the *brāhmaṇas* (intellectuals), the *kṣatriyas* (warriors and adminstrators), the *vaiśyas* (farmers and businessmen), and the *śūdras* (manual laborers). Without the principles of *varṇāśrama-dharma,* human society is almost animal society. Indeed, human civilization begins when human beings accept the four social and spiritual divisions of society, according to quality and work. As Kṛṣṇa says in the *Bhagavad-gītā* (4.13), *cātur-varṇyaṁ mayā sṛṣṭaṁ guṇa-karma-vibhāgaśaḥ:* "I have created the four so-called cial divisions according to quality and work."

In this material world we associate with a particular combination of the modes of nature, and accordingly we mold our character and behavior, and by this criterion we fit into a particular social category. Today people say that there should be no more caste system, but how can they ignore the natural designation of classes in human society? There must be a class of intelligent men, the *brāhmaṇas*, who are qualified to disseminate Vedic knowledge to the people in general. There must be a class of *kṣatriyas* to offer administrative rule and protection. There must be a class of merchants and farmers, the *vaiśyas*, who trade and perform agricultural duties such as cow protection. And there must be a class of *śūdras*, who render service to the other classes. All men fit into these four classes, each according to his *guṇa*, or nature.

Prescribed Duty vs. Unlawful Action

Whatever our *varṇa* or *āśrama*, however, the perfection of our work is to satisfy Viṣṇu, or Kṛṣṇa. The Lord states this in the *Bhagavad-gītā* (3.9):

yajñārthāt karmaṇo 'nyatra
loko 'yaṁ karma-bandhanaḥ
tad-arthaṁ karma kaunteya
mukta-saṅgaḥ samācara

"Work done as a sacrifice for Viṣṇu has to be performed; otherwise work causes bondage in this material world. Therefore, O Arjuna, perform your prescribed duties for His satisfaction, and in that way you will always remain free from bondage." This is the sum and substance of human life. Since we have to work, we should work for Kṛṣṇa. Then we are saved from all sinful reactions.

But if we work for our personal sense gratification, we will become entangled in the reactions, lifetime after lifetime. It is not possible for a person to get out of the clutches of repeated birth and death as long as he continues to pursue sense gratification.

Caitanya Mahāprabhu says, *jīvera 'svarupa' haya—kṛṣṇera 'nitya-dāsa'* (*Caitanya-caritāmṛta, Madhya-līlā* 20.108): "The constitutional position of the living entity is that he is eternally a servant of Kṛṣṇa." If one takes that position, he is saved; otherwise not.

And how does one who accepts his position as a servant of Kṛṣṇa work? Prahlāda Mahārāja explains in the *Śrīmad-Bhāgavatam* (7.5.23):

śravaṇaṁ kīrtanaṁ viṣṇoḥ
smaraṇaṁ pāda-sevanam
arcanaṁ vandanaṁ dāsyaṁ
sakhyam ātma-nivedanam

"Hearing and chanting about the transcendental holy name, form, qualities, paraphernalia, and pastimes of Lord Viṣṇu, remembering these, serving the lotus feet of the Lord, offering the Lord respectful worship, offering prayers to the Lord, becoming His servant, considering the Lord one's best friend, and surrendering everything to Him—these are the nine processes of pure devotional service."

In order to take up these processes seriously, one must accept the regulative principles for spiritual life: no meat-eating, no illicit sex, no intoxication, and no gambling. Then one will be able to accept the injunction to chant the Hare Kṛṣṇa *mahā-mantra* and always be engaged in the service of the Lord in one of the above nine ways. If we accept this authority, our life will be successful, both spiritually and materially. Otherwise, we will have to be satisfied with indulging in sense gratification, performing sinful activities, suffering like dogs and hogs, and enduring repeated birth, old age, disease, and death.

Forgetfulness

We accept the body as our self, thinking, "I am this body." However, we are not the body but rather the owner of the body, just as we are not our apartment but rather the owner or resident of the apartment. The soul is called *dehī*, "one who possesses a body." When we study our body, we say, "This is my hand, this is my leg." We do not say, "I am this hand, I am this leg." Yet the illusion that we are the body persists. The body is nothing but a vehicle for the soul. Sometimes a new motorcar is wrecked in an accident, and the driver is overwhelmed with the sense of loss, forgetting that he is not the motorcar. That is the effect of *ahaṅkāra*, false ego, or false conception of proprietorship.

Because we are covered by ignorance, we have forgotten what our previous body was. Even in this life we do not remember that we were once babies on the laps of our mothers. So many things have happened in our lifetime, but we do not remember them all. If we cannot even remember things that have happened in this life, how can we remember our last life?

A person engages in sinful activities because he does not know what he did in his past life to get his present materially conditioned body, which is subjected to the threefold miseries—those produced by his own body and mind, those caused by other living entities, and those arising from natural disasters. As stated by Lord Ṛṣabhadeva in the *Śrīmad-Bhāgavatam* (5.5.4), *nūnaṁ pramattaḥ kurute vikarma yad indriya-prītaya āpṛṇoti:* a human being who is mad after sense gratification does not hesitate to act sinfully. *Na sādhu manye:* this is not good. *Yata ātmano 'yam asann api kleśada āsa dehaḥ:* because of such sinful actions, one receives another body in which to suffer as he is suffering in his present body because of his past sinful activities.

A person who does not have Vedic knowledge always acts in ignorance of what he has done in the past, what he is doing at the present, and how he will suffer in the future. He is completely in darkness. Therefore the Vedic injunction is *tamasi mā:* "Don't remain in darkness." *Jyotir gama:* "Try to go to the light." This light is Vedic knowledge, which one can understand when one is elevated to the mode of goodness or when one transcends the mode of goodness by engaging in devotional service to the spiritual master and the Supreme Lord.

Knowledge Through Service

How service to the Lord and the spiritual master results in Vedic knowledge is described in the *Śvetāśvatara Upaniṣad* (6.23):

yasya deve parā bhaktir
yathā deve tathā gurau
tasyaite kathitā hy arthāḥ
prakāśante mahātmanaḥ

"Unto those great souls who have implicit faith in both the Lord and the spiritual master, all the imports of Vedic knowledge are automatically revealed." The *Vedas* enjoin, *tad-vijñānārthaṁ sa gurum evābhigacchet:* one must approach a spiritual master who has full knowledge of the *Vedas* and be directed by him in order to become a devotee of the Lord. Then the knowledge of the *Vedas* will be revealed. When the Vedic knowledge is revealed, one need no longer remain in the darkness of material nature.

According to his association with the material modes of nature—goodness, passion, and ignorance—a living entity gets a particular type of body. The example of one who associates with the mode of goodness is a qualified *brāhmaṇa.* Such a *brāhmaṇa* knows past, present, and future because he consults the Vedic literature and sees through the eyes of scripture (*śāstra-cakṣuḥ*). He can understand what his past life was, why he is in the present body, and how he can obtain liberation from the clutches of *māyā* and not accept another material body. This is all possible when one is situated in the mode of goodness. Generally, however, the living entities in this material world are engrossed in the modes of passion and ignorance.

One who is in the mode of ignorance cannot know what

his past life was or what his next life will be; he is simply interested in his present body. Even though he has a human body, a person in the mode of ignorance and interested only in his present body is like an animal, for an animal, being covered by ignorance, thinks that the ultimate goal of life is immediate happiness—to eat and have sex. A human being must be educated to rise above this platform, to understand his past life and how he can endeavor for a better life in the future. There is even a book, called the *Bhṛgu-saṁhitā,* which reveals information about one's past, present, and future lives according to astrological calculations. Somehow or other one must be enlightened about his past, present, and future. One who is interested only in his present body and who tries to enjoy his senses to the fullest extent is understood to be engrossed in the mode of ignorance. His future is very, very dark. Indeed, the future is always dark for one who is covered by gross ignorance. Especially in this age, human society is covered by the mode of ignorance, and therefore everyone thinks his present body to be everything, without consideration of the past or future.

CHAPTER 10

The Next Life: It's Up to Us

The Yamadūtas continued: "O best of the demigods, we can see three different varieties of life, which are due to the contamination of the three modes of nature. The living entities are thus known as peaceful, restless, and foolish; as happy, unhappy, or in-between; or as religious, irreligious, and semireligious. We can deduce that in the next life these three kinds of material nature will similarly act. Just as springtime in the present indicates the nature of springtimes in the past and future, so this life of happiness, distress, or a mixture of both gives evidence concerning the religious and irreligious activities of one's past and future lives.

"The omnipotent Yamarāja is as good as Lord Brahmā, for while situated in his own abode and in everyone's heart like the Paramātmā, he mentally observes the past activities of a living entity and thus understands how the living entity will act in future lives.

"As a sleeping person acts according to the body manifested in his dreams and accepts it to be himself, so one identifies with his present body, which he acquired because of his past religious or irreligious actions, and is unable to know his past or future lives." (*Śrīmad-Bhāgavatam* 6.1.46–49)

Breaking Free of Past, Present, and Future Karma

Here the Yamadūtas point out that the actions and reactions of the three modes of material nature are visible in this life. For example, some people are very happy, some are very distressed, and some are in mixed happiness and distress. This is the result of past association with the modes of material nature—goodness, passion, and ignorance. Since these varieties are visible in this life, we may assume that the living entities, according to their association with the different modes of material nature, will be happy, distressed, or between the two in their next lives also. Therefore the best policy is to disassociate oneself from the three modes of material nature and be always transcendental to their contamination. This is possible only when one fully engages in the devotional service of the Lord, as Kṛṣṇa confirms in the *Bhagavad-gītā* (14.26):

māṁ ca yo 'vyabhicāreṇa
bhakti-yogena sevate
sa guṇān samatītyaitān
brahma-bhūyāya kalpate

"One who engages in full devotional service, unfailing in all circumstances, at once transcends the modes of material nature and thus comes to the level of Brahman." Unless one is fully absorbed in the service of the Lord, one will be subjected to the contamination of the three modes of material nature and must therefore experience distress or mixed happiness and distress, depending on the severity of one's sinful activities.

Changing Bodies

The Supreme Lord has appointed Yamarāja to decide the proper punishment for those who perform sinful activities. Thus at death each being is awarded a particular body in a particular place, according to his work. As Lord Kapila explains in the *Śrīmad-Bhāgavatam* (3.31.1),

karmaṇā daiva-netreṇa
jantur dehopapattaye
striyāḥ praviṣṭa udaraṁ
puṁso retaḥ-kaṇāśrayaḥ

"Under the supervision of the Supreme Lord and according to the result of his work, the living entity, the soul, is made to enter the womb of a woman through the particle of male semen to assume a particular type of body."

We are changing our bodies every day, at every moment. It is called "growth," but actually it is a change of body. Growing means leaving the old body and accepting a new body. After some years we can see that a child has grown to boyhood, then to youth. That means he has changed his body. Similarly, when we find that the body is no longer inhabitable, we have to give it up and accept another body, just as we have to give up our clothes when they become old and worn.

This change is executed under the supervision of higher authorities (*daiva-netreṇa*). According to one's religious and irreligious acts, one has to accept a particular type of body in a particular position and suffer. Our sufferings are classified as *ādhibhautika, ādhyātmika,* and *ādhidaivika. Ādhyātmika* miseries are those caused by our own bodies and minds, *ādhibhautika* miseries are those inflicted by other living entities, and *ādhidaivika* miseries are those which are inflicted by higher authorities (*devas*) and which are completely beyond our control—such as earthquake, drought, flood, and famine. We cannot adjust these situations. In the same way, after death superior authorities will offer us a certain type of body, and we cannot say, "Oh no, sir, I do not want this body." We have to accept it.

Minute Independence

Due to repeated birth and death in so many material bodies, we have all forgotten that we are part and parcel of God, that we have an intimate relationship with Him, and that somehow or other we have fallen into this material world. It is very difficult to exactly pinpoint the origin of this forgetfulness. But even though we have forgotten Him since time immemorial, Kṛṣṇa is so merciful that to remind us of our spiritual identity and our oneness with Him as His parts, He comes personally and teaches us what we have forgotten. And when He departs He leaves behind the scripture, especially the *Bhagavad-gītā,* where He requests, *sarva-dharmān parityajya mām ekaṁ śaraṇaṁ vraja:* "Please give up all your nonsense and surrender unto Me. I shall give you all protection." (*Bhagavad-gītā* 18.66)

Kṛṣṇa is the father of all living entities. He is not happy that all these souls in the material world are rotting like hogs. Therefore He sends His representatives. In the case of Lord Jesus Christ, Kṛṣṇa sent His son. Lord Jesus claimed to be the son of God. Everyone is a son of God, but this son was an especially favorite son, and he was sent to a particular place to reclaim the conditioned souls back home, back to Godhead.

But if the conditioned souls insist on staying here, what can Kṛṣṇa or His servant do? They allow us to go on with our materialistic activities, because the first condition for getting out of the material prison house is that we must desire to get out. When we finally become disgusted with our predicament, we pray, "My dear Lord, I have served lust, anger, and greed for so long, but they are still unsatisfied, and now I have become disgusted with serving them. Now, my dear Lord Kṛṣṇa, my intelligence is awakened, and I have come to You. Please engage me in Your service."

The living entity is the marginal energy (*taṭastha-śakti*) of the Lord, which means he can choose to be controlled by Kṛṣṇa's inferior, material energy or His superior, spiritual energy. We devotees have chosen to come to Kṛṣṇa consciousness. In other words, we have agreed to surrender to Kṛṣṇa and submit to the protection of His internal, spiritual energy. Surrender to Kṛṣṇa begins with chanting the Hare Kṛṣṇa *mantra:* Hare Kṛṣṇa, Hare Kṛṣṇa, Kṛṣṇa Kṛṣṇa, Hare

Hare/ Hare Rāma, Hare Rāma, Rāma Rāma, Hare Hare. The word *Hare* indicates the devotional energy of Kṛṣṇa, *Kṛṣṇa* means "the all-attractive Supreme Personality of Godhead," and *Rāma* means "the Supreme Enjoyer."

But there are many who will not come, because they do not agree to come under the control of Kṛṣṇa's spiritual energy. But Kṛṣṇa does not interfere. He says, "You may remain in the material world or come to Me—whatever you like." We have been given minute independence and the intelligence to discriminate between what to do and what not to do.

Wake Up!

The ear is the most important organ for learning what is to be done and what is not to be done for our ultimate benefit. We must hear from the superior authority. At night we sleep peacefully, unaware that someone might be coming to chop off our head. However, our sense of hearing is acute, even in the sleeping state. If someone cries out, "Wake up! Wake up! Someone is coming to kill you!" we can be saved. Similarly, we are sleeping under the influence of material nature. We seem to be awake and acting, but *prakṛti* (material nature) is doing the acting—not us. We are being forced to act according to our association with the different modes of material nature. Although we are in the sleeping condition, our ear does not sleep, and it helps us to rise out of ignorance. If we hear from the right person—the spiritual master—and from the Vedic scriptures, we can awaken to our original, constitutional position as eternal servants of Kṛṣṇa. The first prescription is *śravaṇam,* hearing about Kṛṣṇa. If we simply hear about Kṛṣṇa, we will automatically wake up. The injunction of the *Vedas* is *uttiṣṭhata jāgrata prāpya varān nibodhata:* "Wake up! Get up! Understand the great benediction you have in this human form of life. Now utilize it and get free from the clutches of the material modes of nature." In the *Bhagavad-gītā* (7.14) Kṛṣṇa explains how to do this:

daivī hy eṣā guṇa-mayī
mama māyā duratyayā
mām eva ye prapadyante
māyām etāṁ taranti te

"This divine energy of Mine, consisting of the three modes of material nature, is difficult to overcome. But those who have surrendered to Me can easily cross beyond it." Surrender to Kṛṣṇa and be Kṛṣṇa conscious. In the human form of life, that is our only business.

CHAPTER 11

The Realm of the Senses

The Yamadūtas continued: "Above the five senses of perception, the five working senses, and the five objects of the senses is the mind, which is the sixteenth element. Above the mind is the seventeenth element, the soul, the living being himself, who, in cooperation with the other sixteen, enjoys the material world alone. The living being experiences three kinds of situations, namely happy, distressful, and mixed.

"The subtle body is endowed with sixteen parts—the five knowledge-acquiring senses, the five working senses, the five objects of sense gratification, and the mind. This subtle body is an effect of the three modes of material nature. It is composed of insurmountably strong desires, and therefore it causes the living entity to transmigrate from one body to another in human life, animal life, and life as a demigod. When the living entity gets the body of a demigod, he is certainly very jubilant, when he gets a human body he is always in lamentation, and when he gets the body of an animal he is always afraid. In all conditions, however, he is actually miserable. His miserable condition is called *saṁsṛti*, or transmigration in material life.

"The foolish embodied living entity, inept at controlling his senses and mind, is forced to act according to the influence of the modes of material nature, even against his desires. He is like a silkworm that uses its own saliva to create a cocoon and then becomes trapped in it, with no possibility of getting out. The living entity traps himself in

a network of his own fruitive activities and then can find no way to release himself. Thus he is always bewildered, and repeatedly he dies.

"No living entity can remain unengaged, even for a moment. One must act by his natural tendency according to the three modes of material nature because this tendency forcibly makes him work in a particular way. The fruitive acts a living being performs, whether pious or impious, are the unseen cause for the fulfillment of his desires. This unseen cause is the root of the living entity's different bodies. Because of his intense desire, the living entity takes birth in a particular family and receives a body like his mother's or father's body. Thus the gross and subtle bodies are created according to his desire.

"Since the living entity is associated with material nature, he is in an awkward position, but if in the human form of life he is taught how to associate with the Supreme Personality of Godhead or His devotee, this position can be overcome." (*Śrīmad-Bhāgavatam* 6.1.50–55)

The Demands of the Senses

These verses describe how the living entity becomes entangled in the material body due to the interaction of the material modes of nature. Everyone engages in work with his hands, legs, and other senses just to achieve a certain goal according to his concocted ideas. In this way one tries to enjoy the five sense objects, namely form, sound, taste, aroma, and touch, not knowing that the actual goal of life is to satisfy the Supreme Lord. Because of disobeying the Lord, the living entity is put into material conditions, and he then tries to improve his situation according to his whims, not caring to follow the instructions of the Supreme Personality of Godhead. Nevertheless, the Supreme Lord is so kind that He comes Himself to instruct the bewildered living entity how to act obediently and then gradually return home, back to Godhead, where he can attain an eternal, peaceful life of bliss and knowledge.

In the material world the living entity has a body that is a very complicated combination of the material elements, and with this body he struggles alone, as indicated in verse 50 by the words *ekas tu.* For example, if one is struggling in the ocean, he must swim through it alone. Although many other men and aquatics are swimming in the ocean, he must take care of himself, because no one else will help him. Therefore this verse indicates that the seventeenth item, the soul, must work alone. Although he tries to create society, friendship, and love, ultimately no one can help him but Kṛṣṇa, the Supreme Lord. Therefore his only concern should be how to satisfy Kṛṣṇa—how to surrender to Him and evoke His mercy. That is also what Kṛṣṇa wants. As He says in the *Bhagavad-gītā* (18.66), *sarva-dharmān parityajya mām ekaṁ śaraṇaṁ vraja:* "Just give up all kinds of concocted religion and surrender to Me."

People bewildered by material conditions try to be united, but although they strive for unity among men and nations, all their attempts are futile. Everyone must struggle alone for existence with the many elements of nature. Therefore one's only hope, as Kṛṣṇa advises, is to surrender to Him, for He can help one become free from the ocean of nescience. Śrī Caitanya Mahāprabhu therefore prayed:

ayi nanda-tanuja kiṅkaraṁ
patitaṁ māṁ viṣame bhavāmbudhau
kṛpayā tava pāda-paṅkaja-
sthita-dhūlī-sadṛśaṁ vicintaya

"O Kṛṣṇa, beloved son of Nanda Mahārāja, I am Your eternal servant, but somehow or other I have fallen into this ocean of nescience, and although I am struggling very hard, there is no way I can save myself. If You kindly pick me up and fix me as one of the particles of dust at Your lotus feet, that will save me."

Similarly, Śrīla Bhaktivinoda Ṭhākura sings, *anādi karama-phale, paḍi' bhavārṇava-jale, taribāre nā dekhi upāya:* "My dear

Lord, I cannot remember when I somehow or other fell into this ocean of nescience, and now I can find no way to rescue myself." We should remember that everyone is responsible for his own life. If an individual becomes a pure devotee of Kṛṣṇa, he is then delivered from the ocean of nescience. Thus his life becomes successful.

Pain and Pleasure

Actually, there is no pleasure in the material world; everything is painful. Everyone is trying to be happy by sensual activity, but the result is unhappiness and frustration. This is called *māyā,* illusion.

Lord Buddha understood the nature of material pleasure. In his youth he was a prince, enjoying great opulence and sensual pleasures, but he renounced it all. Sitting down in meditation, he stopped all sensual activities, which subject one to the pains and pleasures of this material world. He gave up his kingdom just to teach that sensual activities do not help us attain salvation. Salvation means to get out of the clutches of the pleasure and pain of this world.

Buddhism is concerned largely with the predicament of the body. Due to the interactions of the three modes of material nature, which are acting on our material bodies, we experience various pains and pleasures. Buddhism teaches that one can be relieved of these pains and pleasures as soon as one dismantles the combination of the material elements in the shape of the physical body. *Nirvāṇa,* the goal of Buddhism, is the state attained when a person has finished with the material combinations. After all, pains and pleasures are due to possessing this material body. However, Buddhist philosophy does not provide information about the soul, the possessor of the body. Thus Buddhism is imperfect.

Buddhist philosophy is incomplete, but that does not mean Lord Buddha did not know the complete truth. A teacher may have received his Masters degree, yet he still teaches the ABC's to his students. It is not that his knowledge is limited to the ABC's. Similarly, any especially empowered incarnation (*śaktyāveśa avatāra*) will preach God consciousness according to time, place, and circumstances. The teacher holds his Masters degree, but the students may not be qualified to receive the high instructions that the teacher is competent to teach.

Therefore there are different schools of religion, like Buddhism and Śaṅkarācrya's Māyāvāda philosophy. Both the Buddhists and the Māyāvādīs encourage their followers to try to get free of pain and pleasure, which are due to sensual activities. No genuine philosopher urges his followers to pursue sensual activities. Buddha finishes with matter: to achieve *nirvāṇa* one must first dismantle the material combination of the body. In other words, the body is a combination of five material elements: earth, water, fire, air, and ether, and this combination is the cause of all pain and pleasure; so when the combination is at last dismantled, there will be no more pain and pleasure. Śaṅkarācarya's philosophy is to get out of this combination of material elements and become situated in our original, spiritual position. Thus the Māyāvādīs' motto is *brahma satyaṁ jagan mithyā:* "Brahman, the Absolute, is true, and this material creation is false." Śaṅkarācārya rejected Buddha's philosophy, which gives no information concerning the spirit soul. Buddha's philosophy deals only with matter and the dissolution of matter; thus the goal of Buddhism is to merge into the voidness.

Both Buddhism and Māyāvāda philosophy reveal only partial truth. Śaṅkarācārya's Māyāvāda philosophy accepts Brahman, spirit, but does not describe spirit in its fullness. Māyāvāda philosophy teaches that as soon as we become cognizant of our existence as Brahman (*ahaṁ brahmāsmi*), then all our activities come to a stop. But this is not a fact. The living entity is always active. It may seem that in meditation one can stop all sensual activity, but still one is meditating, and that is also action.

While meditating on Brahman, the Māyāvādī thinks, "I

have become God." In one sense, of course, it is correct to think, "I am one with God," for as spirit souls we are all one with God in quality. But no one can ever become *quantitatively* one with God. In the *Bhagavad-gītā* (15.7) Kṛṣṇa declares that the living entities are "part and parcel of Me." Kṛṣṇa is completely spiritual (*sac-cid-ānanda*), so each particle of spirit must also be *sac-cid-ānanda,* just as a gold earring is qualitatively one with the gold in a gold mine. Still, the gold earring is not the gold mine.

So the Māyāvādīs' mistake is to think that the part can become equal to the whole. They presume that because they are part and parcel of God, they *are* God. Therefore the *Śrīmad-Bhāgavatam* (10.2.32) describes the impersonalists as *aviśuddha-buddhayaḥ:* "Their intelligence is impure; they are still in ignorance." Māyāvādīs believe that by accumulating knowledge they become one with God, and thus they address one another as "Nārāyaṇa." That is their great mistake. We cannot become Lord Nārāyaṇa. Nārāyaṇa is *vibhu,* which means "very big" or "infinite," whereas we are *aṇu,* infinitesimal. Our spiritual magnitude measures one ten-thousandth of the tip of a hair. Therefore how can any sane man claim that he has become God?

Śaṇkarācārya gave a hint about Brahman, teaching everyone to think, *ahaṁ brahmāsmi,* "I am the spirit self, not the material body." The *Vedas* agree. One who is situated in *mukti,* or liberation, understands perfectly, "I am not this body; I am pure spirit soul." But that is not the end of self-realization. Next one has to ask, "If I am an eternal spirit soul, what is my eternal spiritual activity?" That eternal activity is devotional service to Kṛṣṇa.

In the *Bhagavad-gītā* (18.54) Lord Kṛṣṇa describes how Brahman realization leads to devotional service:

brahma-bhūtaḥ prasannātmā
na śocati na kāṅkṣati
samaḥ sarveṣu bhūtesu
mad-bhaktiṁ labhate parām

"One who is transcendentally situated at once realizes the Supreme Brahman and becomes fully joyful. He never laments or desires to have anything. He is equally disposed toward every living entity. In that state he attains pure devotional service unto Me."

Often big *svāmīs* talk about attaining "Brahman realization" but do not remove themselves from worldly pleasures and pains. They involve themselves in humanitarian activities, thinking, "My fellow countrymen are suffering; let me open a hospital" or "They are uneducated; let me open a school." If someone is really on the platform of *brahma-bhūtaḥ,* why would he accept any particular place as his country? Actually, as spirit souls we do not belong to any country. We get a body, and as soon as the body is finished, the connection with a particular country is also finished. The symptom of lamentation reveals that the so-called liberated person has not been cured of his attachment to worldly pleasure and pain. That means he has not become joyful, because one who is joyful does not lament. So many learned *sannyāsīs* have fallen down to material activities because they have not in fact realized Brahman. It is not so easy. As already explained, the influence of the modes of nature is very strong. The living entity entangled in different types of fruitive activity is like a silkworm trapped in a cocoon. Getting free is very difficult unless one is helped by the Supreme Personality of Godhead.

Spiritual Senses

Real knowledge is attained by applying the senses in the service of Kṛṣṇa. At present, our mind and senses are absorbed in bodily designations, such as "I am American," "I am Indian," or "I am English." In this consciousness we think that we should apply our senses in the service of our relatives, our society, our nation, etc. But these are temporary circumstances. Our real position is that we are Brahman, pure spirit soul. As long as we think of ourselves as belonging to some temporary designation, we cannot become a devotee of Kṛṣṇa.

As we have pointed out, Brahman realization is not the end of spiritual knowledge. There are three stages of self-realization: Brahman, or the realization that one is not this body but a spirit soul; Paramātmā realization, or understanding the Lord within the heart; and Bhagavān realization, realizing the Lord in His personal form as Śrī Kṛṣṇa.

Beyond Brahman is Paramātmā realization, realizing Kṛṣṇa in the heart as Supersoul. Brahman is like the sunlight, but Paramātmā realization is like seeing the sun globe itself, the source of the sun's rays. Going still further, one can enter into the spiritual planets of Vaikuṇṭha and see the Supreme Personality of Godhead face to face. This is the ultimate stage of self-realization and is like meeting the sun-god himself. The sunlight, the sun globe, and the sun-god are one and inseparable, yet they are simultaneously different. The sunlight is the impersonal effulgence of the sun, the sun globe is its localized aspect, and the sun-god is the personal source of both the sun globe and the sunlight. In the *Bhagavad gītā* (14.27) Kṛṣṇa confirms that He is the source of the Brahman effulgence: *brahmaṇo hi pratiṣṭhāham.* "I am the basis of the impersonal Brahman." And in the *Īśopaniṣad* (15) a devotee prays,

hiraṇmayena pātreṇa
satyasyāpihitaṁ mukham
tat tvaṁ pūṣann apāvṛṇu
satya-dharmāya dṛṣṭaye

"O my Lord, sustainer of all that lives, Your real face is covered by Your dazzling effulgence. Please remove that covering and exhibit Yourself to Your pure devotee."

So Brahman realization is not enough. A sick man's fever may go down, but he may not yet be cured. He is finally cured when he is not only safe from fever but fully recovered and back to his normal, active life. Otherwise there is danger of relapse. Likewise, understanding "I am a spirit soul, not the body" does not mean one is cured of illusion. Only when a person fully understands that he is the eternal servant of Kṛṣṇa and he acts on that understanding is he truly self-realized.

A Special Concession for All People

In the present age, for all people the best path to achieve self-realization is to chant the Hare Kṛṣṇa *mahā-mantra*: Hare Kṛṣṇa, Hare Kṛṣṇa, Kṛṣṇa Kṛṣṇa, Hare Hare/ Hare Rāma, Hare Rāma, Rāma Rāma, Hare Hare. The conditioned souls in this Age of Kali are so engrossed in sinful activities that it is impossible for them to follow the Vedic injunctions in a systematic way. The chanting of the Hare Kṛṣṇa *mahā-mantra* is the special concession of Śrī Caitanya Mahāprabhu—Kṛṣṇa Himself—who appeared five hundred years ago just to deliver the fallen souls by inaugurating the *saṅkīrtana* movement, the movement of the congregational chanting of the Lord's holy names. Lord Caitanya would often quote the following verse from the *Bṛhan-nāradīya Purāṇa* (3.8.126):

harer nāma harer nāma
harer nāmaiva kevalam
kalau nāsty eva nāsty eva
nāsty eva gatir anyathā

"In this age the only way to attain salvation is to chant the holy name, chant the holy name, chant the holy name of the Lord. There is no other way, no other way, no other way."

We can see the power of chanting the holy name of Kṛṣṇa by studying the Kṛṣṇa consciousness movement. In this movement all kinds of sinful activities are being given up by persons who have been addicted to bad habits ever since they were living in the wombs of their mothers. This is their good fortune. As Śrī Caitanya Mahāprabhu says in the *Caitanya-caritāmṛta* (*Madhya-līlā* 19.151),

brahmāṇḍa bhramite kona bhāgyavān jīva
guru-kṛṣṇa-prasāde pāya bhakti-latā-bīja

"The living entity is rotating in different lives and in different bodies, transmigrating from one situation to another throughout the universe, but if he is fortunate and gets the mercy of Kṛṣṇa, he will get a bona fide spiritual master, from whom he will receive the seed of the creeper of *bhakti,* devotional service." If he is truly intelligent, he will sow that seed in his heart and water it. If you sow a seed in the earth, you must water it so that it will fructify. Similarly, once the seed of *bhakti* has been sown in the heart, it has to be watered properly. What is that water? *Śravaṇaṁ kīrtanam:* hearing and chanting the glories of Kṛṣṇa is the watering process that will make the seed of devotional service grow.

By cultivating devotional service to Kṛṣṇa, we can get out of our unfortunate position in the material world, which Kṛṣṇa has certified in the *Bhagavad-gītā* as *duḥkhālayam,* a place full of miseries. In other words, by taking shelter of the lotus feet of Kṛṣṇa in the shape of chanting and hearing His holy name, we will not have to undergo repeated birth and death in this miserable material world.

Body of Desire

The *Śrīmad-Bhāgavatam* describes in detail how a conditioned living entity takes birth. According to his *karma,* the living entity is put into the semen of a particular father, and the living entity's gross material body is manifested from the union of father and mother. During sexual intercourse, the mentalities of the father and mother are combined when the father's semen and mother's egg mix, and this combination is acquired by the child.

Each of us has a different type of body: no one's body is identical to anyone else's. The different types of bodies have a cause, and that cause is *karma.* According to one's previous activities, one develops a certain kind of subtle body—made up of mind, intelligence, and false ego—and on the basis of the subtle body one gets a particular gross body. As Lord Kṛṣṇa states in the *Bhagavad-gītā* (8.6):

yaṁ yaṁ vāpi smaran bhāvaṁ
tyajaty ante kalevaram
taṁ tam evaiti kaunteya
sadā tad-bhāva-bhāvitaḥ

"Whatever state of being one remembers when he quits his body, O son of Kuntī, that state he will attain without fail." The character of the subtle body at the time of death is determined by the sum total of one's activities during one's lifetime. If a human being is taught to change his subtle body by developing Kṛṣṇa consciousness, at the time of death his subtle body will create a gross body in which he will be a devotee of Kṛṣṇa—or if he is still more advanced, he will not take another material body at all but will immediately get a spiritual body and thus return home, back to Godhead. This is the perfection of human life.

CHAPTER 12

Bewildered by Desire

The Yamadūtas continued: "In the beginning this *brāhmaṇa* named Ajāmila studied all the Vedic literatures. He was a reservoir of good character, good conduct, and good qualities. Firmly established in executing all the Vedic injunctions, he was very mild and gentle, and he kept his mind and senses under control. Furthermore, he was always truthful, he knew how to chant the Vedic *mantras*, and he was also very pure. Ajāmila was very respectful to his spiritual master, the fire-god, guests, and the elders of his household. Indeed, he was free from false prestige. He was upright, benevolent to all living entities, and well behaved. He would never speak nonsense or envy anyone.

"Once Ajāmila, following the order of his father, went to the forest to collect fruit, flowers, and two kinds of grass, called *samit* and *kuśa*. On the way home he came upon a lusty fourth-class man (*śūdra*) shamelessly embracing and kissing a prostitute. The *śūdra* was smiling, singing, and enjoying as if this were proper behavior. Both the *śūdra* and the prostitute were drunk. The prostitute's eyes were rolling in intoxication, and her dress had become loose. Such was the condition in which Ajāmila saw them.

"The *śūdra*, his arm decorated with turmeric powder, was embracing the prostitute. When Ajāmila saw her, the dormant lusty desires in his heart awakened, and in illusion he fell under their control. As far as possible he patiently tried to remember the instructions of the *śāstras* not even to see a woman. With the help of this knowledge

and his intellect, he tried to control his lusty desires, but because of the force of Cupid within his heart, he failed to control his mind." (*Śrīmad-Bhāgavatam* 6.1.56–62)

Brahminical Qualifications

The order-carriers of Yamarāja, the Yamadūtas, are explaining the factual position of piety and impiety and how a living entity is entangled in this material world. Describing the history of Ajāmila, the Yamadūtas relate that in the beginning he was a learned scholar of the Vedic literature. He was well behaved, neat and clean, and very kind to everyone. In fact, he had all good qualities. In other words, he was a perfect *brāhmaṇa*. A *brāhmaṇa* is expected to be perfectly pious, to follow all the regulative principles, and to have all good qualities. The symptoms of piety are explained in these verses.

Apparently Ajāmila followed the rules and regulations of celibacy as a perfect *brahmacārī* and was very softhearted, truthful, clean, and pure. How he fell down in spite of all these qualities and thus came to be threatened with punishment by Yamarāja is described here.

Because Ajāmila was born into a *brāhmaṇa* family, he was naturally *śruta-sampanna*. *Śruta* means that by hearing the *Vedas*, Ajāmila was rich in Vedic knowledge. In India *brāhmaṇas* are called *paṇḍitas*, "learned men." A *brāhmaṇa* cannot be a fool and a rascal. Therefore one who has no knowledge of the *Vedas* cannot be a *brāhmaṇa*. Simply reading the *Vedas* from a scholastic viewpoint is useless. One must practically apply the knowledge of the *Vedas*. Armchair Vedāntists smoke cigarettes while reading *Vedānta*, but that kind of study is useless. We have seen many so-called *sannyāsīs* talking on *Vedānta*, smoking all the while. Ajāmila was not that type. He was a scholar of Vedic literature, and he was very well behaved. A *brāhmaṇa* must study the *Vedas* under the guidance of a spiritual master, and after the purificatory process of *upanāyana-saṁskāra*, he becomes *dvija*, or twice-born. At that time the sacred thread is offered to such a person. This is the sign by which we can understand a person has formally accepted a spiritual master. It is a kind of badge.

One who is not twice-born is unqualified to understand the *Vedas.* It is not that just because one happens to know a little Sanskrit he becomes expert in Vedic knowledge. Many foreign scholars have translated the *Vedas,* but we do not accept their translations as bona fide, because a student of the *Vedas* must be *dvija.* When a person has become truthful, able to control his mind and senses, clean, simple and tolerant, full of knowledge, and able to practically apply knowledge in life, and when he has full faith in God, Kṛṣṇa, he is *dvija.* Such a person can be said to have become a duly qualified *brāhmaṇa,* and he is able to study and understand the *Vedas.*

Ajāmila was not only born in a *brāhmaṇa* family, but he was qualified in Vedic knowledge. In his youth he studied the *Vedas* completely. He was *śīlavān,* "very gentle." He was also *sad-ācāra,* which means he observed the habit of keeping clean and rising early in the morning to attend Vedic temple ceremonies, such as *maṅgala-ārati.* He was a reservoir of good qualities. We too can be *sad-ācāra* if we practice devotional service regularly, including daily attendance at *maṅgala-ārati* and chanting sixteen rounds of the Hare Kṛṣṇa *mantra* on beads. These practices will gradually cleanse us of material contamination.

Upon accepting initiation from the spiritual master, one takes a vow to perform these spiritual activities daily. Even the six Gosvāmīs of Vṛndāvana, who were liberated personalities, regularly chanted the *mahā-mantra* many times daily, and they never failed to offer their obeisances to the Deity and the devotees. Raghunatha dāsa Gosvāmī would offer obeisances flat on the ground (*daṇḍavats*) many times daily. These activities indicate that the Gosvāmīs were *dhṛta-vrata,* accustomed to taking vows with great determination and carrying them out. Without practicing austerity and penance with firm determination, we cannot approach

God. One who is serious about making spiritual advancement has to accept all these regulative principles.

Ajāmila possessed all brahminical qualifications, and he knew all the necessary *mantras*, such as the Gāyatrī *mantra* and the Hare Kṛṣṇa *mahā-mantra*. Also, he was always rendering service to his *guru*. That is the first qualification of a *brāhmaṇa*. In Vedic times, every high-caste family performed a fire sacrifice in the morning after taking a bath and chanting Vedic *mantras*. *Agni* (the sacrificial fire) was continually lit. They offered oblations to the fire, to the *guru*, and then to all the adult members of the family. Thus they daily offered respect to their father and mother and to the spiritual master. Nowadays this is not done, but in the Vedic system this was the first business of the day.

A good example of this practice of respecting elders is Yudhiṣṭhira Mahārāja, the great saintly Pāṇḍava king. After the battle of Kurukṣetra, Yudhiṣṭhira and his four brothers would go every day to offer their respects to their paternal uncle, Dhṛtarāṣṭra. Dhṛtarāṣṭra had contrived many plots to destroy the Pāṇḍavas, finally declaring war on them, but the result was that every one of his hundred sons died. Even after he lost the war, he still refused to welcome his nephews, the sons of his brother Pāṇḍu. This was a great insult to King Yudhiṣṭhira. One day Dhṛtarāṣṭra's younger brother, Vidura, a great Vaiṣṇava, went to Dhṛtarāṣṭra and said, "My dear brother, you are so shameless that first you declare war against the Pāṇḍavas, and now that you are an old man, still you do not receive King Yudhiṣṭhira as your guest, yet you live in his house at his expense. Are you so shameless, my dear brother?" Vidura spoke in this way just to help Dhṛtarāṣṭra break his attachment to family life. Dhṛtarāṣṭra was an old man, and all his sons were dead, but still he sat in his household arrangement, eating nicely prepared food. From this we can understand that family attachment is very strong. Vidura chastised Dhṛtarāṣṭra: "You are coughing up mucus because you are very old, and your liver is weak. You will die very soon, yet you are still sitting in your comfortable chair, just like a dog. Have you no more shame than a dog, which always sits waiting for his master to feed him?"

Upon hearing Vidura's harsh words, Dhṛtarāṣṭra's hard heart softened, and he replied,"Yes! My dear brother Vidura, please let me know what I should do."

Vidura said, "Come with me immediately to the forest. For the remaining days of your life, just engage yourself in Kṛṣṇa consciousness. Come with me." So without telling anyone, Dhṛtarāṣṭra left with Vidura, and Gāndhāri, Dhṛtarāṣṭra's faithful wife, followed. Together they went to the forest to finish their life in meditation on the Lord.

When King Yudhiṣṭhira came to offer his obeisances in the morning and saw that his uncles were not there, he became anxious, considering that Dhṛtarāṣṭra was an old man. At that time the great sage Nārada Muni appeared and informed him, "Do not worry. Dhṛtarāṣṭra and his wife, Gāndhāri, have been brought to the forest by your uncle Vidura."

This story from the *Śrīmad-Bhāgavatam* illustrates the system of offering respects to the elderly members of the family. After the morning's duties are performed, next one must go and offer obeisances to the spiritual master and the elderly persons in the family. One must also offer respects to a guest. Usually we know when a certain guest is coming to our home and can make preparations beforehand, but sometimes it happens that someone comes unexpectedly, and he too must be received with respect. And when it comes to eating, the head of the family should feed the older members first, then his children and other members of the family. He will eat last, and before he eats his food he should stand in the road and call out, "If anyone is hungry, please come. I still have not taken my food, and you are welcome!" Some remnants of food should be kept at home in anticipation of unexpected guests. The Vedic principle is that when someone comes and begs, "Sir, I am hungry," a man must give the hungry guest his own food even if he himself remains hungry. That is real *gṛhastha-āśrama.* I have seen that a young man will not smoke in the presence of an old man without permission, even if they are strangers. So a young man will show consideration even to an older stranger, what to speak of his father or elder brother. In Vedic society, any older man is offered respect. These principles are not hard and fast, but this is Vedic custom.

Thus Ajāmila was trained in his youth to offer respect to the spiritual master and his elders. This is one of the symptoms of *sad-ācāra.* Gentleness is another symptom. In other words, he was friendly to all living beings. A real *brāhmaṇa* is the friend of everyone, even an ant.

In this regard there is a story about Nārada Muni and a hunter. Once Nārada Muni was passing through a forest near Prayag and saw that many animals were lying half-dead. Feeling compassion for the suffering creatures, he cried out, "Who is the culprit who is killing these animals, leaving them to die in this way?"

The barbaric hunter Mṛgāri answered, "Dear sage, please let me do my business. If you have come here to beg for a deerskin, I shall give it to you."

But Nārada said, "I haven't come to beg anything from you, but to ask why you are only half-killing these animals. It is a great sin. It is better that you kill them outright."

Mṛgāri replied, "My father taught me to kill them like this. I did not know it is sinful."

Nārada said, "Yes, it is very sinful. You will have to suffer very much for it."

The hunter became thoughtful and asked, "What should I do?"

Nārada Muni advised him, "Give up this nonsense business."

Mṛgāri protested, "Then how shall I eat?"

But Nārada Muni said, "I shall provide you with food."

The hunter agreed, "All right, if you give me food, I can give up this business."

Nārada Muni then requested Mṛgāri to sit down on the bank of the Ganges and chant Hare Kṛṣṇa before a sacred *tulasī* plant. Nārada Muni went to the nearby village and announced that a pure Vaiṣṇava was now chanting nearby on the bank of the Ganges. Upon seeing Mṛgāri sitting and chanting peacefully, the village people said to one another, "He has given up his hunting business and is chanting Hare Kṛṣṇa." They began coming regularly to the bank of the Ganges to visit Mṛgāri. Someone brought rice, someone brought *dāl*, and someone else brought fruit. The food began to pile up.

The hunter Mṛgāri wondered, "Why is Nārada Muni sending me so much food? I have only myself and my wife to maintain." Thus he began distributing the food. Chanting Hare Kṛṣṇa and distributing *prasādam* daily, he became a perfect Vaiṣṇava. (This is the system introduced in this Kṛṣṇa consciousness movement—chanting the Hare Kṛṣṇa *mahā-mantra* and distributing *prasādam.* In every temple of Kṛṣṇa we do this.)

After some time, Nārada Muni called upon his friend Pārvata Muni and said, "I have a very nice disciple who was a hunter. Let us go and see how he is doing." Pārvata Muni agreed. When the two sages approached Mṛgāri's house, they saw that he was jumping this way and that. Upon seeing Nārada Muni, he prepared to offer obeisances at his feet, but before he did so he took the edge of his *dhotī* and gently brushed away the ants crawling on the ground so as not to crush them. He had been jumping because he was trying to avoid stepping on the ants. This was the very man who a short time before had been tormenting all kinds of animals, yet now he was not prepared to kill even an ant. That is the nature of a Vaiṣṇava.

So, Ajāmila had this quality of gentleness, which is prominent in *brāhmaṇas.* Also, despite all his training, Ajāmila was not proud. He was free of *ahaṅkāra,* or false ego. The very word *ahaṅkāra* means "I am doing this, I am doing that, and therefore I have become so big." Ajāmila was free of this attitude. Nor was he envious. In these degraded times, everyone is envious of one or more persons. But *brāhmaṇas* like Ajāmila are free of this propensity. Only when one has acquired these brahminical qualities and is accustomed to brahminical habits can one expect to be liberated from material bondage.

Ruined by Sex Attraction

Unfortunately, as related in these verses, Ajāmila lost his brahminical status. Once, as a young man, Ajāmila went to collect flowers and other articles for Deity worship. His father ordered him, "Bring all these things from the forest." While coming back, Ajāmila came upon a fourth-class man and a prostitute, who are vividly described here. Drunkenness was sometimes manifest even in bygone ages, although not very frequently. In the present Age of Kali, however, such sin is to be seen everywhere, for people all over the world have become shameless. Long ago, when Ajāmila saw the scene of the drunken *śūdra* and the prostitute, he was affected, although up until then he had been a perfect *brahmacārī.* Nowadays promiscuity is visible in so many places, and we must consider the position of a *brahmacārī* student who sees such behavior. For such a *brahmacārī* to remain steady is very difficult unless he is extremely strong in following the regulative principles. Nevertheless, one who takes to Kṛṣṇa consciousness very seriously can withstand the provocation of sin.

In our Kṛṣṇa consciousness movement we prohibit illicit sex, intoxication, meat-eating, and gambling. In Kali-yuga, a drunken, half-naked woman embracing a drunken man is a very common sight, especially in the Western countries, and restraining oneself after seeing such things is very difficult. Nevertheless, if by the grace of Kṛṣṇa a man adheres to the regulative principles and chants the Hare Kṛṣṇa *mantra,* Kṛṣṇa will certainly protect him. Indeed, Kṛṣṇa says that His devotee is never vanquished (*kaunteya pratijānīhi na me bhaktaḥ praṇaśyati*). Therefore all the disciples practicing Kṛṣṇa consciousness should obediently follow the regulative principles and remain fixed in chanting the holy name of the Lord. Then there need be no fear. Otherwise one's position is very dangerous.

Ajāmila had vowed to follow the regulative principles of spiritual life. But as we see, even when one is highly qualified there is the chance of a fall. Seeing the low-class couple engaged in public sex proved to be his downfall. Everyone knows that a husband and wife have sexual intercourse, but this should be done privately. Sex in public is animalistic. Similarly, sex with many partners is illicit. Nowadays illicit sex is common throughout the world, especially in the Western countries. A young girl thinks, "I will find a suitable man, attract him, and have sex, but I won't marry him right away. I will test this man, then that man. When I have found the one who makes me happy, then I will marry." This is the mentality of a prostitute. And similarly, the young boys are hunting for many sex partners. These are commonplace activities in Western countries, where the boys and girls receive no spiritual training.

In such a cat-and-dog society, there can be no peace. All the leaders talk about peace, and they meet in peace conferences, but there can be no peace from conferring and passing resolutions. There cannot be peace unless the whole social structure is reformed, and that can be done only by Kṛṣṇa consciousness.

Kṛṣṇa consciousness is cultivated by good association, just as a degraded mentality is a result of bad association. As Lord Ṛṣabhadeva says in the *Śrīmad-Bhāgavatam* (5.5. 2), *mahat-sevāṁ dvāram āhur vimuktes tamo-dvāraṁ yoṣitāṁ saṅgi-saṅgam:* "If we want to open the door to liberation, we should engage ourselves in the service of the *mahātmās,* the pure devotees, but if we want to open the door to hellish life, then we can associate with those who are very attached to women." The lusty people of today's so-called civilized society do not care for Kṛṣṇa consciousness. They do not care for their elderly family members. They indulge in sex in the street, on the beach, in the cinema. Sex is advertised constantly to attract the attention of the people. In this way materialistic atheists add fuel to the fire of lust, and people are going to hell.

So, Ajāmila became degraded by seeing a low-class couple embracing. Because both the *śūdra* and the prostitute were drunk, their eyes were rolling, and the prostitute's clothes were loose. Nowadays it has become fashionable to wear revealing clothing, but this practice is abominable. It simply makes the body more attractive for sex indulgence. It is said that if one's body is smeared with turmeric, it increases the lusty desires of the opposite sex. The word *kāma-liptena* indicates that the *śūdra* was decorated with turmeric smeared on his body. Because the *śūdra* and the prostitute were rascals, they were not ashamed. They exhibited themselves freely, not caring for public criticism. They were laughing, smiling, singing, and embracing, and the young Ajāmila saw everything when he passed by on the road.

In modern times sexual affairs of this kind are regularly shown in the cinema, and thus it is not hard to guess what kind of character is forming in the young men and women of today. By seeing these activities only once, Ajāmila fell down. In this way Ajāmila's spiritual education and training were finished. He was stunned and bewildered. When Cupid attacks, all one's education, culture, and knowledge are lost. Therefore one has to avoid this free-mixing, lusty society. Cāṇakya Paṇḍita advises, "Always avoid associating with persons too attached to sense gratification. Rather, associate with those who are engaged in the devotional activities of spiritual life." For this reason boys are sent to the *gurukula,* the house of the bona fide spiritual master, who trains them in spiritual life from the age of five.

Unless one is very strong in knowledge, patience, and proper bodily, mental, and intellectual behavior, controlling one's lusty desires is extremely difficult. Thus after seeing a man embracing a young woman and practically doing everything required for sex, even a fully qualified *brāhmaṇa*, as described above, could not control his lusty desires and restrain himself from pursuing them. Because of the force of materialistic life, to maintain self-control is extremely difficult unless one is specifically under the protection of the Supreme Personality of Godhead through devotional service.

CHAPTER 13

Ajāmila Begins His Degraded Life

The Yamadūtas continued: "In the same way that the sun and moon are eclipsed by a low planet, the *brāhmaṇa* Ajāmila lost all his good sense. Thus he always thought of the prostitute, and within a short time he took her as a servant in his house and abandoned all the regulative principles of a *brāhmaṇa*.

"Ajāmila began spending whatever money he had inherited from his father to satisfy the prostitute with various material presentations so that she would remain pleased with him. He gave up all his brahminical activities to satisfy her. Because his intelligence was pierced by her lustful glance, Ajāmila engaged in sinful acts in her association. He even gave up the company of his extremely beautiful young wife, who came from a respectable *brāhmaṇa* family.

"This rascal Ajāmila, although born of a *brāhmaṇa* family, lost his intelligence because of the prostitute's association, and thus he earned money somehow or other, regardless of whether properly or improperly, and used it to maintain her and her children. In this way he spent his long lifetime transgressing all the rules and regulations of the holy scripture, living extravagantly, and eating food prepared by a prostitute. Therefore he is full of sins. He is unclean and is addicted to forbidden activities.

"Ajāmila did not undergo atonement. Therefore because of his sinful life, we must take him into the presence

of Yamarāja for punishment. There, according to the extent of his sinful acts, he will be punished and thus purified." (*Śrīmad-Bhāgavatam* 6.1.63–68)

We Must Serve . . . But Whom?

As mentioned before, Ajāmila was trained as a proper *brāhmaṇa* from birth, and thus he was properly situated in service to his spiritual master, elders like his father, and the Supreme Personality of Godhead. But due to his association with a prostitute, he gave up his brahminical engagements and became a servant of Lord Kṛṣṇa's illusory energy, *māyā.*

There are two kinds of servants: *māyā's* servants and Kṛṣṇa's servants. Every living entity is originally a servant of Kṛṣṇa. Lord Caitanya Himself affirms this: *jīvera 'svarūpa' haya—kṛṣṇera 'nitya dāsa.'* "The constitutional position of the living entity is to be an eternal servant of Kṛṣṇa." (*Caitanya-caritāmṛta, Madhya-līlā* 20.108) In this world, everyone is trying to be a master. Individually and collectively, everyone is trying to assert, "I am the lord of all I survey." But this attitude is futile, because by nature everyone is a servant. Instead of becoming a servant of Kṛṣṇa, we have become the servant of our senses. In either case we are servants. Therefore, those who are really intelligent think, "If I have to work as a servant, why not be a servant of Kṛṣṇa?" Only the Kṛṣṇa conscious devotee is sane, because he accepts his natural position as a servant of Kṛṣṇa.

Worship of Lord Kṛṣṇa, or Viṣṇu, is the actual goal of Vedic civilization, but the so-called Vedāntists do not accept this. They divert their attention to the worship of demigods and advise that one may worship any of them. No! Even demons (*asuras*) sometimes worship demigods. Rāvaṇa was a great devotee of Lord Śiva, but he was an *asura.* Similarly, Hiraṇyakaśipu was a great devotee of Lord Brahmā, but he was also an *asura.* Anyone who is not a devotee of Lord Viṣṇu is an *asura.* That is the verdict of the *Vedas.* Ajāmila was a *brāhmaṇa,* which means that he was a servant of Nārāyaṇa. In other words, he was a Vaiṣṇava.

A Vaiṣṇava is one who recognizes that Lord Kṛṣṇa is the supreme proprietor and enjoyer, and that everyone else is His servant. Just as the master is the enjoyer of his entire establishment, so Kṛṣṇa is the enjoyer of everything and everyone in both the material and spiritual worlds. Actually, no one else is the enjoyer—no one else is in the position to enjoy. Kṛṣṇa is the only enjoyer.

When we forget our relationship with Kṛṣṇa as His eternal servitors, we become servants of our senses. Following the dictation of our senses, we enter into the darkest regions of illusion and are subjected to the punishment of Yamarāja. Sometimes our conscience forbids us, "Don't do this," but we surrender to our lust and greed, and thus we do it anyway. Kṛṣṇa is within our heart, also dictating "Don't do it," yet still we do it. This kind of service to our senses simply brings suffering. Since we must serve, why not serve Kṛṣṇa? Why should we serve our senses, which are never satisfied anyway? We should become servants of God; that is the perfection of life. Otherwise we shall be obliged to become servants of our senses and suffer.

One who becomes a servant of Kṛṣṇa becomes a *gosvāmī*, a master of his senses. The title "Gosvāmī" indicates one who refuses to follow the dictations of his senses. Instead he follows the dictation of the Supreme Personality of Godhead, just as Rūpa Gosvāmī and Sanātana Gosvāmī did. "Gosvāmī" is not a caste title. Before becoming a *gosvāmī*, Rūpa Gosvāmī served the Mohammedan government as a minister and was consequently rejected by the Hindu *brāhmaṇa* society. But when he gave up the dictation of Nawab Hussain Shah to follow the dictation of Caitanya Mahāprabhu, the Lord made him a *gosvāmī*.

All genuine *gosvāmīs* are also *vairāgīs*, renunciants. But if one is unable to be a real *vairāgī*, then he must become a *gṛhastha* (householder). It is not that one may pose himself as a *brahmacārī* or a *sannyāsī* and at the same time indulge in illicit sex secretly. That is abominable. If a genuine householder practices *karma-yoga*, giving the results of his activities to Kṛṣṇa, he will eventually attain the platform of perfect renunciation. He should not desire to enjoy the fruits of his activities but should instead work as a matter of duty, thinking "Kṛṣṇa wants this—Kṛṣṇa will be satisfied by my doing this—and therefore I must do it." This is the right attitude for a devotee. Arjuna was unwilling to fight for his personal interest, but when he understood that Kṛṣṇa wanted him to fight, he took it as his duty: "It must be done. It does not matter whether I like it or not. Kṛṣṇa wants it, and therefore I must do it." That is the attitude of a renounced devotee of the Lord.

In the *Bhagavad-gītā* (18.66) Lord Kṛṣṇa instructs His disciple Arjuna, "Just surrender unto Me, and I shall protect you from all sinful reactions." And Arjuna accepts Kṛṣṇa's instruction with the words *kariṣye vacanaṁ tava:* "I will do as You say." (*Bhagavad-gītā* 18.73) If we follow Arjuna's example, we will be in direct contact with Kṛṣṇa, and we will be able to surmount all difficulties in both our spiritual and material life. We hear the instructions of Kṛṣṇa via the unbroken chain of disciplic succession (*guru-paramparā*). Acceptance of these instructions is called *śikṣā,* or voluntarily following the instruction of the spiritual master. The independent nature of the living entity is that he does not want to follow the instructions of another living being, however pure. But when one voluntarily agrees to obey the orders of the spiritual master, one is following the orders of Kṛṣṇa, and thus one's life becomes perfect.

In the *Śrīmad-Bhāgavatam* (11.17.27) Kṛṣṇa says,

ācāryaṁ māṁ vijānīyān
nāvamanyeta karhicit
na martya-buddhyāsūyeta
sarva-deva-mayo guruḥ

"One should know the *ācārya* as Myself and never disrespect him in any way. One should not envy him, thinking him an ordinary man, for he is the representative of all the demigods." Thinking the spiritual master an ordinary person and envying him are causes of a devotee's falling down. Devotional service requires training under the guidance of a spiritual master, and this guidance is received when one surrenders to the spiritual master, inquires from him, and renders service to him. But these are impossible for one who envies the spiritual master.

Ruined by a Prostitute . . . Saved by the Holy Name

Ajāmila was trained as a *brāhmaṇa,* but he lost his position as a *brāhmaṇa* by associating with a prostitute, so much so that he forgot all his brahminical activities. Nevertheless, at the end of his life, by chanting the four syllables of the holy name Nārāyaṇa, he was saved from the gravest danger of falling down. As Kṛṣṇa says in the *Bhagavad-gītā* (2.40), *svalpam apy asya dharmasya trāyate mahato bhayāt:* "Even a little devotional service can save one from the greatest danger." Devotional service, which begins with chanting the holy name of the Lord, is so powerful that even if a person falls down from the exalted position of a *brāhmaṇa* through sexual indulgence, he can be saved from all calamities if he somehow or other chants the holy name of the Lord. This is the extraordinary power of the Lord's holy name. Therefore in the *Bhagavad-gītā* it is advised that one not forget the chanting of the holy name even for a moment: *satataṁ kīrtayanto māṁ yatantaś ca dṛḍha-vratāḥ.*

There are so many dangers in this material world that one may fall down from an exalted position at any time. Yet if one keeps himself always pure and steady by chanting the Hare Kṛṣṇa *mahā-mantra,* he will be safe without a doubt. Ajāmila did not do this, and therefore he lost all his brahminical qualities by the association of a prostitute. Especially mentioned here is the effect of eating food prepared by a prostitute. Food prepared by an unclean, sinful woman is extremely infectious. Ajāmila ate such food, and therefore he became sinful.

Also mentioned here is Ajamila's misuse of his inheritance. Customarily everyone is eligible to inherit his father's property, and Ajāmila also inherited the money of his father. But what did he do with the money? Instead of engaging the money in the service of Kṛṣṇa, he engaged it in the service of a prostitute. Therefore he was condemned. How did this happen? He was victimized by the prostitute's dangerous, lustful glance.

A chaste and faithful wife will give birth to good sons, who will then offer oblations to their forefathers and thus deliver them if by chance they have fallen into a hellish condition. The very word *putra* ("son") means "one who can deliver his forefathers from hell." Śrī Caitanya Mahāprabhu showed this by His example when He went to Gayā to offer oblations to His forefathers. Even today there is a Viṣṇu temple in Gayā where such oblations are offered at the lotus feet of Lord Viṣṇu. There have been cases where one's father or mother took the body of a ghost at death, and after oblations were offered at the lotus feet of Lord Viṣṇu at Gayā, the father or mother was delivered. However, anyone who becomes a Vaiṣṇava offers oblations to Viṣṇu at every moment, and thus his forefathers are automatically delivered. If one son in the family becomes a Vaiṣṇava, he can deliver fourteen generations of ancestors and fourteen generations of yet unborn descendants. This is confirmed in the *Śrīmad-Bhāgavatam.*

As sense control is the beginning of pious life, illicit sex is the beginning of sinful life. One should not engage in illicit sex, or sex for any reason except having a child with one's wife. Marriage is meant for begetting children, and in that sense it is a religious institution. Lord Kṛṣṇa confirms this in the *Bhagavad-gītā* (7.11): *dharmāviruddho bhūteṣu kāmo 'smi.* "I am sex that does not contradict religious principles." Caitanya Mahāprabhu had a devotee named Śivānanda Sena, who was a family man. Śivānanda used to come with all the devotees every year to see Lord Caitanya in Purī, and he came together with his wife and children.

Once he came to see the Lord, and his wife offered her respects. At that time she was pregnant, so Caitanya Mahāprabhu advised Śivānanda, "This time when you get your child, you should give him the name Paramānanda dāsa." Caitanya Mahāprabhu knew that pregnancy resulted from sex, but He did not condemn sex in this case, as it was conducted according to scriptural injunction.

On the other hand, there is the case of Junior Haridāsa. He was a *sannyāsī,* a renunciant, who was an intimate associate of the Lord. Once he merely desired sex and did not actually partake of it, and immediately Caitanya Mahāprabhu, in His Paramātmā feature, could understand this. The Lord then asked His other associates not to allow Junior Haridāsa to come before Him anymore. Sarvabhauma Bhattācārya, Rāmānanda Rāya, and other intimate associates of Caitanya Mahāprabhu requested, "Junior Haridāsa is Your eternal servant. Somehow or other he has committed this offense, but kindly excuse him." Still, Lord Caitanya Mahāprabhu was firm in this respect and immediately replied, "If you like Junior Haridāsa so much, better you remain with him, and I will go away." From that moment, nobody ventured again to request Caitanya Mahāprabhu to excuse Junior Haridāsa. When Junior Haridāsa became hopeless in his efforts to be excused by Caitanya Mahāprabhu, he went to Prayag and drowned himself in the confluence of the rivers Yamunā and Ganges. Although Lord Caitanya knew about this incident, after some time He inquired of His associates, "Where is Junior Haridāsa now?"

They replied, "Sir, You did not accept him, and so he has committed suicide."

Lord Caitanya said, "Yes, very good. This is very good."

Caitanya Mahāprabhu was sometimes harder than stone and sometimes softer than a flower. That is the behavior of the Supreme Personality of Godhead. Śivānanda was a bona fide *gṛhastha,* obeying the rules and regulations of householder life, whereas Junior Haridāsa merely desired sex, but because he was in the renounced order of life he was condemned. A *sannyāsī* gives up his family and takes a vow to abstain from sex, but if he again takes to sex he commits a very great sin.

So, Ajāmila was victimized by illicit sex with a prostitute. There are many instances throughout the world in which even a purified person falls victim to attraction by a prostitute and spends all his money on her. Prostitute-hunting is so abominable that sex with a prostitute can ruin one's character, destroy one's exalted position, and plunder all one's money. Therefore illicit sex is strictly prohibited. One should be satisfied with his married wife, for even a slight deviation will create havoc. A Kṛṣṇa conscious *gṛhastha* should always remember this. He should always be satisfied with one wife and be peaceful simply by chanting the Hare Kṛṣṇa *mantra*. Otherwise at any moment he may fall down from his good position, as exemplified by the case of Ajāmila.

Considering the abominable character of Ajāmila, the Yamadūtas were perplexed as to why the Viṣṇudūtas had forbidden them to take such a man to Yamarāja for punishment. Since Ajāmila had not undergone atonement for his sinful acts, the Yamadūtas thought he should be taken to Yamarāja to be purified. Punishment by Yamarāja is a process of purification for the most abominable sinful persons. Therefore the Yamadūtas requested the Viṣṇudūtas not to obstruct their taking Ajāmila to Yamarāja.

CHAPTER 14

Betrayed by Leaders

Śukadeva Gosvāmī said: My dear king, the servants of Lord Viṣṇu are always very expert in logic and argument. After hearing the statements of the Yamadūtas, the Viṣṇudūtas replied as follows:

"Alas, how painful it is that irreligion is being introduced into an assembly where religion should be maintained! Indeed, those in charge of maintaining religious principles are needlessly punishing a sinless, unpunishable person.

"A king or government official should be so well qualified that he acts as a father, maintainer, and protector of the citizens because of affection and love. He should give the citizens good advice and instructions according to the standard scriptures and should be equal to everyone. Yamarāja does this, for he is the supreme master of justice, and so do those who follow in his footsteps. However, if such persons become polluted and exhibit partiality by punishing an innocent person, where will the citizens go to take shelter for their maintenance and security?

"The mass of people follow the example of a leader and imitate his behavior. They accept as evidence whatever the leader accepts. People in general are not very advanced in knowledge by which to discriminate between religion and irreligion. The innocent, unenlightened citizen is like an ignorant animal sleeping in peace with its head on the lap of its master, faithfully believing in the master's protection. If a leader is actually kindhearted and deserves to be the object of a living entity's faith, how can he punish or kill a

foolish person who has fully surrendered in good faith and friendship?" (*Śrīmad-Bhāgavatam* 6.2.1–6)

Logic and Reason

The Viṣṇudūtas, like all genuine servants of God, understood everything according to logic and reason. The instructions of Kṛṣṇa are not meaningless dogma. Religion often gives rise to dogmatism, but the author of *Śrī Caitanya-caritāmṛta,* Śrīla Kṛṣṇadāsa Kavirāja, urges us to try to understand Lord Caitanya and the philosophy of Kṛṣṇa consciousness according to logic. In other words, do not follow blindly, on the basis of sentiment alone. One who fails to apply logic can easily be misled by unscrupulous persons. For example, some so-called missionaries advertise that man can become God, and they attract millions of sentimental followers. But how is it possible? Where is there evidence of any man becoming God? This false propaganda is not at all logical. One should use his intelligence to understand Kṛṣṇa consciousness.

However, once we have accepted the philosophy of Kṛṣṇa consciousness and taken initiation from a bona fide spiritual master, we cannot argue with him. We cannot challenge. To do so would constitute an offense and a fall from spiritual principles.

The Duty of Governments

The Viṣṇudūtas accused the Yamadūtas of violating religious principles by attempting to drag Ajāmila to Yamarāja for punishment. Yamarāja is the officer appointed by the Supreme Personality of Godhead to judge religious and irreligious principles and to punish the sinful. However, if completely sinless people are punished, the entire assembly of Yamarāja is contaminated. This principle applies not only in the assembly of Yamarāja but throughout human society.

Upholding religious principles is the duty of the king or government. Unfortunately, in the present age, Kali-yuga, people have lost their intelligence, so they cannot differentiate between *dharma* and *adharma,* religion and irreligion. The courts do not know whom to punish and whom not. For example, out of compassion for all the fallen souls, Vaiṣṇavas go out to preach the principles of Kṛṣṇa consciousness, but unfortunately, because of the influence of Kali-yuga, even though these Vaiṣṇavas have dedicated their lives to preaching the glories of the Lord, they are sometimes harassed and punished by courts on false charges of disturbing the peace. This age, Kali-yuga, is very bad. We can only take shelter of Kṛṣṇa and always chant Hare Kṛṣṇa, Hare Kṛṣṇa, Kṛṣṇa Kṛṣṇa, Hare Hare/ Hare Rāma, Hare Rāma, Rāma Rāma, Hare Hare.

The Viṣṇudūtas chastised the Yamadūtas for violating the principles of justice. Such corruption of the judicial system is very prominent in Kali-yuga. The judicial system is meant to provide for execution of justice, yet false witnesses and bribery make it difficult. With money, almost anyone can get a favorable judgment in court. If the justice system is corrupt, life becomes extremely troublesome. The government is supposed to offer the citizens protection, as parents do for their children. A small child is completely dependent on his father and mother, thinking with full faith, "My father is here, my mother is here—I am safe." But if the father and mother are corrupt, where is the protection for the child? Similarly, if the whole government is corrupt, where is the protection for the citizens?

Whatever the heads of society do, people generally follow. The government or king is like a father to the citizens. A father will never tolerate the killing or injuring of his children. He will give up his own life trying to attack the person threatening his children. Yet today crime is rampant. The government spends billions of dollars, but the citizens have no security in their lives. The government is answerable to the citizens because it must protect and provide for them. If the government is incapable or corrupt, then what is the position of the citizens?

The king, or in modern times the government, should act as the guardian of the citizens by teaching them the proper goal of life. The human form of life is especially meant for attaining self-realization, realization of one's relationship with the Supreme Personality of Godhead. The duty of the government, therefore, is to take charge of training all the citizens in such a way that they will gradually be elevated to the spiritual platform and realize their relationship with God. This principle was followed by kings like Mahārāja Yudhisthira, Mahārāja Parīkṣit, Lord Rāmacandra, Mahārāja Ambarīṣa, and Prahlāda Mahārāja.

Unfortunately, today's government leaders are generally dishonest and irreligious, and thus all the affairs of the state suffer. In the name of democracy, rogues and thieves fool the innocent populace into electing them to the most important posts in the government. Recently this has been proven in America, and as a result the citizens condemned the President and dragged him down from his post. This is only one case out of many.

In Kali-yuga, people have no shelter. Due to corrupt government, they are uncertain of their lives and property. The mass of people should always feel secure because of the government's protection. Therefore, how regrettable it is for the government itself to cause a breach of trust and put the citizens in difficulty for political reasons. We saw during the partition days in India that although Hindus and Muslims had been living together peacefully, manipulation by politicians suddenly aroused feelings of hatred between them, and thus the Hindus and Muslims killed one another over politics. This is a sign of Kali-yuga.

Another symptom of Kali-yuga is the abominable practice of animal slaughter. In this age animals are kept nicely sheltered, completely confident that their masters will protect them, but unfortunately as soon as the animals are fat, they are immediately sent for slaughter. Such cruelty is condemned by Vaiṣṇavas like the Viṣṇudūtas. Indeed, hellish conditions of extreme suffering await the sinful men responsible for such cruelty. One who betrays the confidence of a living entity who takes shelter of him in good faith, whether that living entity be a human being or an animal, is extremely sinful. Because such betrayals now go unpunished by the government, all of human society is terribly contaminated. The people of this age are therefore described as *mandāḥ sumanda-matayo manda-bhāgyā hy upadrutāḥ.* As a consequence of such sinfulness, men are condemned (*mandāḥ*), their intelligence is unclear (*sumanda-matayaḥ*), they are unfortunate (*manda-bhāgyāḥ*), and therefore they are always disturbed by many problems (*upadrutāḥ*). This is their situation in this life, and after death they are punished in hellish conditions.

Although Ajāmila was not punishable, the Yamadūtas were insisting on taking him away to Yamarāja for punishment. This was *adharma,* contrary to religious principles. The Viṣṇudūtas feared that if such irreligious acts were allowed, the management of human society would be spoiled. In modern times, the Kṛṣṇa consciousness movement is trying to introduce the right principles of management for human society, but unfortunately the governments of Kali-yuga do not properly support the Hare Kṛṣṇa movement because they do not appreciate its valuable service. The Hare Kṛṣṇa movement is the right movement for ameliorating the fallen condition of human society, and therefore governments and public leaders in every part of the world should support this movement to completely rectify humanity's sinful condition.

CHAPTER 15

Atonement

The Viṣṇudūtas continued: "Ajāmila has already atoned for all his sinful actions. Indeed, he has atoned not only for sins performed in one life but for those performed in millions of lives, for in a helpless condition he chanted the holy name of Nārāyaṇa. Even though he did not chant purely, he chanted without offense, and therefore he is now pure and eligible for liberation.

"Even previously, while eating and at other times, Ajāmila would call his son, saying, 'My dear Nārāyaṇa, please come here.' Although calling the name of his son, he nevertheless uttered the four syllables *nā-rā-ya-ṇa.* Simply by chanting the name of Nārāyaṇa in this way, he sufficiently atoned for the sinful reactions of millions of lives.

"The chanting of the holy name of Lord Viṣṇu is the best process of atonement for one who steals gold or other valuables, for a drunkard, for one who betrays a friend or relative, for one who kills a *brāhmaṇa*, or for a man who indulges in sex with the wife of his *guru* or another superior. It is also the best method of atonement for a man who murders his father, the king, or women, for one who slaughters cows, and for all other sinful men. Simply by chanting the holy name of Lord Viṣṇu, such sinful persons attract the attention of the Supreme Lord, who then considers, 'Because this man has chanted My name, My duty is to give him protection.'" (*Śrīmad-Bhāgavatam* 6.2.7–10)

Absolute Absolution

The Viṣṇudūtas charged that the Yamadūtas did not know whom to arrest and whom not to arrest. The Yamadūtas regularly arrest sinful persons, but in this case the Yamadūtas came to arrest Ajāmila, who had been released from all sinful reactions simply by chanting "Nārāyaṇa!" The Viṣṇudūtas criticized the Yamadūtas, saying, "You do not know whom to punish and whom not to punish. Even though Ajāmila committed so many sinful activities, he is now freed from the reactions to his sins. He has completely counteracted all those sins by chanting the holy name of Nārāyaṇa. Why are you now attempting to arrest this person as if he were a criminal? Although he had no intention of chanting the holy name, still he has chanted it, and therefore he is now free of sin."

The Yamadūtas had considered only the external situation of Ajāmila. Since he was extremely sinful during his life, they thought he should be taken to Yamarāja. They did not know that he had become free from the reactions of all his sins. The Viṣṇudūtas thus instructed them that because he had chanted the name Nārāyaṇa at the time of his death—and also throughout his life—he was freed from all sinful reactions. In this regard Śrīla Viśvanātha Cakravartī Ṭhākura quotes the following verses from the scriptures:

nāmno hi yāvatī śaktiḥ
pāpa-nirharaṇe hareḥ
tāvat kartuṁ na śaknoti
pātakaṁ pātakī naraḥ

"Simply by chanting one holy name of Hari, a sinful man can counteract the reactions to more sins than he can commit." (*Bṛhad-viṣṇu Purāṇa*)

avaśenāpi yan-nāmni
kīrtite sarva-pātakaiḥ
pumān vimucyate sadyaḥ
siṁha-trastair mṛgair iva

"If one chants the holy name, even in a helpless condition or without desiring to do so, all of one's sinful reactions immediately depart, just as a lion's roar causes the small animals in the forest to flee in fear." (*Garuḍa Purāṇa*)

sakṛd uccāritaṁ yena
harir ity akṣara-dvayam
baddha-parikaras tena
mokṣāya gamanaṁ prati

"A person who once chants the holy name of the Lord, consisting of the two syllables *ha-ri*, guarantees his path to liberation." (*Skanda Purāṇa*)

These are some verses explaining why the Viṣṇudūtas stopped the Yamadūtas from taking Ajāmila to Yamarāja.

There are different kinds of sins, one of which is stealing. Thieves and burglars are very sinful. Another sinful activity is drunkenness. Those who are addicted to intoxication and stealing are condemned by the Viṣṇudūtas. Other examples of sins are being unfaithful to one's friends, killing a *brahmaṇa* or Vaiṣṇava, dishonoring one's spiritual master or teacher, killing a woman, killing a king, and killing a cow. These are among the worst sins. But the Viṣṇudūtas say that even though a person has committed many such sins, if he utters the holy name of Nārāyaṇa even once, he at once becomes free from sinful reactions.

Śrīdhara Svāmī says, "Chanting the holy name of Nārāyaṇa, Lord Hari, not only counteracted all of Ajāmila's sinful reactions, but it made him eligible to become liberated, and therefore at the time of death he was transferred to the spiritual world." Chanting the holy name of Kṛṣṇa counteracts all sins—more than one can possibly commit. Because Ajāmila had chanted the holy name without offense, and because he chanted sincerely, he completely freed himself from all sinful reactions. This is why we are stressing the chanting of Hare Kṛṣṇa so much. Pious activities, austerity, sacrifice—everything is done simply by chanting the Hare Kṛṣṇa *mantra.*There is no need of any other process of *yoga,* atonement, or austerity and penance. Simply by chanting without offense one achieves the results of all other ritualistic performances prescribed in the *Vedas.*

Previously, when engaged in sinful activities to maintain his family, Ajāmila chanted the name of Nārāyaṇa, but he did so without offense. To chant the holy name of the Lord just to counteract one's sinful activities, or to commit sinful activities on the strength of chanting the holy name, is offensive (*nāmno balād yasya hi pāpa-buddhiḥ*). But although Ajāmila engaged in sinful activities, he never chanted the holy name of Nārāyaṇa to counteract them; he simply chanted the name Nārāyaṇa to call his son. Therefore his chanting was effective. Because he chanted the holy name in this way, he had already vanquished the accumulated sinful reactions of many, many lives. The conclusion is that one who always chants the holy name of the Lord without offense is always pure. As confirmed in these verses, Ajāmila was already sinless, and because he chanted the name of Nārāyaṇa he remained sinless. It did not matter that he was calling his son; the name itself was effective.

Foolish persons say that one can chant any name, even a demigod's name, and get the same result as chanting the holy name of the Lord. This is Māyāvāda philosophy. The Māyāvādīs think that everyone is God; they say, "The demigods are God, I am God, you are God." Therefore they say one can chant any name and become liberated. In Bengal it is very popular to hold a *kālī-kirtana.* A party of people meet and chant, "Kālī! Kālī! Kālī!" or the names of so many so-called *avatāras.* One rascal added his wife's name to the chanting, and his foolish followers accepted it. In this way Māyāvādī philosophers are leading their followers straight to hell. Caitanya Mahāprabhu has therefore strongly warned against hearing from the Māyāvādī philosophers, lest one's spiritual life be spoiled and the path of devotional service blocked. We should always remember this when there is any question of chanting other names. We should chant the holy name of Viṣṇu, the holy name of Kṛṣṇa—no one else's name.

The scriptures advise us to chant only the name of the Supreme Personality of Godhead, Kṛṣṇa. There are thousands of names of Viṣṇu, and in once sense Kṛṣṇa and Viṣṇu are the same, yet the scriptures explain that chanting a thousand names of Viṣṇu gives the result of chanting the name Rāma just once, and chanting Rāma three times gives the result of chanting Kṛṣṇa once. In other words, one automatically gets all good results just by chanting the holy name of Kṛṣṇa.

Caitanya Mahāprabhu therefore recommends this chanting process, according to śāstric injunction:

harer nāma harer nāma
harer nāmaiva kevalam
kalau nāsty eva nāsty eva
nāsty eva gatir anyathā

"In this age of quarrel and hypocrisy, the only means of deliverance is chanting the holy name of the Lord. There is no other way. There is no other way. There is no other way." (*Bṛhan-nāradīya Purāṇa*)

By taking up this chanting process, we are immediately freed from all sinful reactions. Thus we begin our spiritual life. Without being freed from sinful life, there is no possibility of becoming a pure Vaiṣṇava.

Offenses Against the Holy Name

Even a devotee may sometimes commit some sinful activity, either unknowingly or due to past sinful behavior. But if he sincerely repents, thinking, "I should not have done this, but I am so sinful that I have again committed this sin," the Supreme Lord will excuse him on the basis of his genuine repentance. However, if he intentionally commits sinful activities, expecting that the Lord will forgive him because he is chanting Hare Kṛṣṇa, that is inexcusable.

If one commits sinful activities on the strength of chanting the holy name, he commits *nāma-aparādha*, or an offense against the holy name. Of the ten kinds of offenses, committing sins on the strength of chanting is the most serious. If after being freed from all sinful reactions by chanting Hare Kṛṣṇa one again commits the same sins, he is guilty of a grievous crime. For an ordinary man, that sinful activity may not be regarded so seriously, but for one who is chanting Hare Kṛṣṇa, it is a dangerous offense, just as it is a serious crime for a government officer in a high post to take advantage of his position and accept a bribe. Such men are the most punishable criminals. If a policeman steals, his crime and subsequent punishment are greater than that of an ordinary man who steals. That is the law. Similarly, one who takes gross advantage of the Hare Kṛṣṇa *mantra,* thinking, "I am chanting Hare Kṛṣṇa, so even if I commit some sin I'll be excused," will not achieve the ultimate goal of chanting the holy name. He becomes entangled in a cycle: he is freed, then he again commits sin, then he is freed and again commits sin, freed and again commits sin. In this way he is never liberated.

Nevertheless, one should not think that one's sinful reactions will fail to be counteracted by the chanting of Hare Kṛṣṇa. One of the ten offenses against the holy name of the Lord is to think that the holy name cannot eradicate sinful reactions. Those who cultivate offenseless chanting of the Hare Kṛṣṇa *mahā-mantra* should have firm faith in the words of the *śāstra* that declare the chanting of the holy names of Kṛṣṇa to be supremely powerful. As the Viṣṇudūtas say here, "The chanting of the holy name of Lord Viṣṇu is the best process of atonement for all kinds of sinners." But very often the difficulty is that one will chant Hare Kṛṣṇa and again commit sin.

The Perfection of Chanting

The key to successful chanting, therefore, is to carefully avoid sin altogether. By chanting the Hare Kṛṣṇa *mahā-*

mantra, a person is freed from all reactions to his previous sins, and if he avoids sinning again, he very quickly becomes an advanced devotee. His mind becomes fixed upon the lotus feet of Kṛṣṇa. If we regularly chant Hare Kṛṣṇa without offense, we shall remain free from all sinful reaction, and our attachment for the Supreme Lord in devotional service will increase.

Once there was an argument between Ṭhākura Haridāsa and an ignorant so-called *brāhmaṇa* concerning the power of the holy name of Kṛṣṇa. In an assembly of Vaiṣṇavas, Haridāsa Ṭhākura said, "Not only does a person become situated on the spiritual platform (*brahma-bhūtaḥ*) by offenselessly chanting the holy names of the Lord, but his dormant love of Godhead manifests and he becomes liberated automatically."

The *brāhmaṇa* protested, "Don't exaggerate the effects of chanting in this way. One becomes liberated only after performing many austerities and penances. But you say that simply by chanting Hare Kṛṣṇa one becomes liberated. If that is not the case, I shall certainly cut off your nose."

Haridāsa Ṭhākura replied, "If chanting Hare Kṛṣṇa does not produce liberation as a by-product, then *I* shall cut off my nose."

The members of the assembly witnessing this argument became extremely agitated upon seeing the great offense the *brāhmaṇa* had committed against Haridāsa Ṭhakura, and they immediately expelled the offender. Shortly thereafter, the *brāhmaṇa* contracted leprosy, and his beautiful nose melted away. This incident is narrated in *Śrī Caitanya-caritāmṛta.*

There are three stages of chanting the holy name: chanting with offense, chanting as a liberated person, and chanting with full love of God. These progressive stages of chanting are like the ripening of a mango. An unripe mango tastes sour, but when the fruit is fully ripened, it tastes very sweet. Initially we may be reluctant to chant, but when we become liberated the chanting is so sweet that we cannot give it up. In this regard, Śrīla Rūpa Gosvāmī has composed a beautiful verse describing the sweetness of the holy name of Kṛṣṇa:

tuṇḍe tāṇḍavinī ratiṁ vitanute tuṇḍāvalī-labdhaye
karṇa-kroda-kaḍambinī ghaṭayate karṇārbudebhyaḥ spṛhām
cetaḥ-prāṅgaṇa-saṅginī vijayate sarvendriyāṇāṁ kṛtiṁ
no jāne janitā kiyadbhir amṛtaiḥ kṛṣṇeti varṇa-dvayī

"I do not know how much nectar the two syllables *Kṛṣ-ṇa* have produced. When we chant the holy name of Kṛṣṇa, it appears to dance within the mouth, and we then desire many, many mouths. When the name of Kṛṣṇa enters the holes of the ears, we desire many millions of ears. And when the holy name dances in the courtyard of the heart, it conquers the activities of the mind, and therefore all the senses become inert."

These are the symptoms of one who is on the liberated platform of chanting. At that stage, called *prema*, one has a great relish for chanting Hare Kṛṣṇa, Hare Kṛṣṇa, Kṛṣṇa Kṛṣṇa, Hare Hare/ Hare Rāma, Hare Rāma, Rāma Rāma, Hare Hare. But this stage is attainable only if one follows the regulative principles. We have to be cautious. After being cured of a diseased condition, we first enter the convalescent stage. If we do something wrong, the disease may return. It is not that we become liberated and can do anything and everything. At all times we have to stick by the regulative principles of devotional life.

Accumulated Benefits from Chanting the Holy Name

Śrīla Viśvanātha Cakravartī Ṭhākura provides additional insight into the power of the holy name in his commentary to verses 9 and 10. He writes this commentary in the form a dialogue concerning how one can become free from all sinful reactions simply by chanting the holy name of the Lord:

"Someone may say, 'It may be accepted that by chanting

the holy name of the Lord one becomes freed from all the reactions of sinful life. However, if a person commits sinful acts in full consciousness, not only once but many, many times, he is unable to free himself from the reactions of such sins even after atoning for them for twelve years or more. How is it possible, then, that simply by once chanting the holy name of the Lord one immediately becomes freed from the reactions of such sins?'"

Viśvanātha Cakravartī Ṭhākura replies by quoting verses 9 and 10 of this chapter: "'The chanting of the holy name of Lord Viṣṇu is the best process of atonement for one who steals gold or other valuables, for a drunkard, for one who betrays a friend or relative, for one who kills a *brāhmaṇa,* or for a person who indulges in sex with the wife of his *guru* or another superior. It is also the best method of atonement for a person who murders his father, the king, or women, for one who slaughters cows, and for all other sinful men. Simply by chanting the holy name of Lord Viṣṇu, such sinful persons attract the attention of the Supreme Lord, who then considers, "Because this man has chanted My holy name, My duty is to give him protection."'"

"One may atone for sinful life and vanquish all sinful reactions by chanting the holy name, and this is beyond ordinary atonement. Ordinary atonement may temporarily protect a sinful person, but it does not completely cleanse his heart of the deep-rooted desire to commit sinful acts. Therefore atonement is not as powerful as the chanting of the holy name of the Lord. In the *śāstras* it is said that if a person only once chants the holy name and completely surrenders unto the lotus feet of the Lord, the Lord immediately considers him His ward and is always inclined to give him protection. This is confirmed by Śrīdhara Svāmī. Thus when Ajāmila was in great danger of being carried off by the order-carriers of Yamarāja, the Lord immediately sent His personal order-carriers to protect him, and because Ajāmila was freed from all sinful reactions, the Viṣṇudūtas spoke on his behalf.

"Ajāmila had named his son Nārāyaṇa, and because he loved the boy very much, he would call him again and again. Although he was calling for his son, the name itself was powerful, because the name Nārāyaṇa is not different from Lord Nārāyaṇa. When Ajāmila named his son Nārāyaṇa, all the reactions of his sinful life were neutralized, and as he continued calling his son and thus chanting the holy name of Nārāyaṇa thousands of times, he was actually unconsciously advancing in Kṛṣṇa consciousness.

"One may argue, 'Since Ajāmila was constantly chanting the name of Nārāyaṇa, how was it possible for him to be associating with a prostitute and thinking of wine?' By his sinful actions he was bringing suffering upon himself again and again, and therefore one may say that only his chanting of the holy name of Nārāyaṇa at the time of death—and not his chanting during his lifetime—was the cause of his being freed. However, his chanting during his life would then have been a *nāma-aparādha. Nāmno balād yasya hi pāpa-buddhiḥ:* one who continues to act sinfully and tries to neutralize his sins by chanting the holy name of the Lord is a *nāma-aparādhī,* an offender to the holy name.

"In response it may be said that Ajāmila's chanting throughout his life was inoffensive because he did not chant the name of Nārāyaṇa with the purpose of counteracting his sins. He was in so much illusion that he did not realize he was addicted to sinful actions, nor did he know that his chanting of the holy name Nārāyaṇa was neutralizing them. Thus during his life he did not commit a *nāma-aparādha,* and his repeated chanting of the holy name of Nārāyaṇa while calling his son may be called pure chanting.

"Because of this pure chanting, Ajāmila unconsciously accumulated the results of *bhakti,* devotional service. Indeed, even his first utterance of the holy name was sufficient to nullify all the sinful reactions of his life. To cite a logical example, a fig tree does not immediately yield fruits, but in time the fruits are available. Similarly, Ajāmila's devotional service grew little by little, and therefore although he committed very sinful acts, the reactions did not affect him. In the *śāstras* it is said that if one chants the holy name of the Lord even once, the reactions of past, present, or future sinful life do not affect him. To give another example, if one extracts the poison fangs of a serpent, this saves the serpent's future victims from poisonous effects, even if the serpent bites repeatedly. Similarly, if a devotee chants the holy name even once inoffensively, this protects him eternally. He need only wait for the results of the chanting to mature in due course of time."

CHAPTER 16

Awakening Love of God

The Viṣṇudūtas continued: "By following the Vedic ritualistic ceremonies or undergoing atonement, sinful men do not become as purified as by once chanting the holy name of Lord Hari. Although ritualistic atonement may free one from sinful reactions, it does not awaken devotional service, unlike the chanting of the Lord's names, which reminds one of the Lord's fame, qualities, attributes, pastimes, and paraphernalia.

"The ritualistic ceremonies of atonement recommended in the religious scriptures are insufficient to cleanse the heart absolutely because after atonement one's mind again runs toward material activities. Consequently, for one who wants liberation from the fruitive reactions of material activities, the chanting of the Hare Kṛṣṇa *mantra*, or glorification of the name, fame, and pastimes of the Lord, is recommended as the most perfect process of atonement because such chanting completely eradicates the dirt from one's heart.

"At the time of death, Ajāmila helplessly and very loudly chanted the holy name of Nārāyaṇa. That chanting alone has already freed him from the reactions of all sinful life. Therefore, O servants of Yamarāja, do not try to take him to your master for punishment in hellish conditions.

"One who chants the holy name of the Lord is immediately freed from the reactions of unlimited sins, even if he chants the holy name jokingly, for musical entertainment, neglectfully, or even to indicate something else. This is accepted by all learned scholars of the scriptures.

"If a person somehow or other chants the holy name of Hari while dying because of an accident, such as falling from the top of a house, slipping and suffering broken bones while traveling on the road, being bitten by a snake, being afflicted with pain and high fever, or being injured by a weapon, he is immediately absolved from having to enter hellish life, even if he was sinful throughout his life.

"Learned scholars and sages have carefully ascertained that one should atone for the heaviest sins by undergoing a heavy process of atonement and one should atone for lighter sins by undergoing lighter atonement. But chanting the Hare Kṛṣṇa *mantra* vanquishes all the effects of sinful activities, regardless of whether heavy or light.

"Although one may neutralize the reactions of sinful life through austerity, charity, vows, and other such methods, these pious activities cannot uproot the material desires in one's heart. However, one who serves the lotus feet of the Personality of Godhead is immediately freed from all such contaminations.

"As a fire burns dry grass to ashes, so the holy name of the Lord, whether chanted knowingly or unknowingly, unfailingly burns to ashes all the reactions of one's sinful activities.

"Even if a person is unaware of the potency of a certain medicine, if he takes that medicine or is forced to take it, it will act even without his knowledge, for its potency does not depend on the patient's understanding. Similarly, even though one does not know the value of chanting the holy name of the Lord, if one chants the holy name—knowingly or unknowingly—the chanting will be very effective."

Śrī Śukadeva Gosvāmī continued speaking to King Parīkṣit: My dear king, having thus perfectly judged the principles of devotional service with reasoning and arguments, the order-carriers of Lord Viṣṇu released the *brāhmaṇa* Ajāmila from the bondage of the Yamadūtas and saved him from imminent death. Then the Yamadūtas

went to Yamarāja and explained to him everything that had happened.

The *brāhmaṇa* Ajāmila was now free from fear, having been released from the nooses of Yamarāja's servants. Coming to his senses, he immediately offered obeisances to the Viṣṇudūtas by bowing his head at their lotus feet. He was extremely pleased by their presence, for he had seen them save his life from the hands of the servants of Yamarāja. But when the Viṣṇudūtas saw that Ajāmila was attempting to say something, they suddenly disappeared from his presence. (*Śrīmad-Bhāgavatam* 6.2.11–23)

Atonement vs. Chanting the Holy Name

Here the Viṣṇudūtas say that the Vedic scriptures recommend various means of atonement, by which a person may be delivered from the reactions of his sinful activities. In Christianity there is also a means of atonement. If a Catholic commits a sin, for example, he is instructed to go to a priest and confess: "I have committed such-and-such sin." The priest is supposed to be an authorized representative of God, and so if he excuses the sinner, the sin becomes nullified.

However, such atonement cannot purify the sinful man as much as the purifying process of chanting the holy name of Lord Kṛṣṇa. The man who confesses to having sinned leaves the church and often commits the same sin again. In other words, there is no question of becoming purified by this process of atonement.

Still, atonement of various kinds is recommended in the *Vedas* for those who are not ready to take up the process of pure devotional service. These methods of atonement are proportional to the the severity of the sin they are meant to counteract. For example, if we fall sick with a cough or influenza, the cost of medicine prescribed by the doctor may be little, but if we are stricken with tuberculosis, the medicine will be more costly. Likewise, *prāyaścitta,* or the ritualistic ceremonies for counteracting sinful activities, is proportionately less or greater according to the gravity of the sin. If we commit a grievous sin, then the penance will be severe. These are the prescriptions given by great sages like Parāśara Muni and Manu. The sages have composed twenty kinds of scriptures, constituting the *dharma-śāstra,* and these scriptures are meant for atoning for one's sins and elevating one to the heavenly planets. For example, it is said that if one has committed certain crimes, he must vow to fast for a certain number of days or give charity. Or, a businessman who has earned a million dollars by sinful activities must give in charity accordingly.

There are many such prescribed methods of atonement, but here the Viṣṇudūtas say, "Although these prescribed methods of atonement are authorized and true, they cannot purify the heart." We can see that even though the adherents of Hinduism, Mohammedanism, and Christianity perform such rituals of atonement, they cannot refrain from again committing the same sins. One who practices these principles of atonement is like a rascal patient who goes to a physician for treatment. The physician gives him medicine and instructs him how to take it, but the foolish patient takes the medicine according to his own whims, and so his condition worsens. Again he goes to the physician, crying "Doctor, please give me more medicine."

In this regard, Śrīla Viśvanātha Cakravartī Ṭhākura describes an incident that took place when Sāmba, one of Lord Kṛṣṇa's sons, was rescued from the punishment of the Kauravas. Sāmba fell in love with Lakṣmaṇā, the daughter of Duryodhana, and since according to *kṣatriya* custom one is not offered a *kṣatriya's* daughter unless he displays his chivalrous valor, Sāmba abducted her. Consequently Sāmba was arrested by the Kauravas. Later, when Lord Balarāma came to rescue him, there was an argument about Sāmba's release. Since the argument was not settled, Balarāma showed His power in such a way that all of Hastināpura trembled and would have been vanquished as if by a great earthquake. Then the matter was settled, and Sāmba married Duryodhana's daughter. The purport is that one should take shelter of Kṛṣṇa and Balarāma, whose protective power is so great that it cannot be equaled in the material world. However powerful the reactions of one's sins, they will immediately be vanquished if one chants the name of Hari, Kṛṣṇa, Balarāma, or Nārāyaṇa.

Therefore such rituals of atonement as fasting and giving charity are not accepted by the Viṣṇudūtas. They say, "Such prescribed ritualistic ceremonies cannot purify a man as effectively as chanting the holy name of God." Undoubtedly one becomes free from all contamination of sinful life by executing particular religious principles, but these are ultimately insufficient, because the mind is so disturbed that even after being freed from the contamination of sinful reactions, the mind again becomes attracted to sinful activity.

The purificatory power of devotional service to Kṛṣṇa, beginning with the chanting of the holy name, is stated in the *Śrīmad-Bhāgavatam* (11.2.42): *bhaktiḥ pareśānubhavo viraktir anyatra ca.* "Devotional service to the Lord is so powerful that one who performs it is immediately freed from all material desires." All desires within this material world are sinful because material desire means sense gratification, which always involves action that is more or less sinful. But pure devotional service is *anyābhilāṣitā-śūnya,* free from material desires. One who is situated in devotional service no longer has material desires, and thus he is beyond sinful life. Material desires should be completely stopped. Otherwise, although one's austerities, penances, and charity may free one from sin for the time being, one's desires will reappear because his heart is impure. Thus he will act sinfully and suffer. The special advantage of devotional service is that it frees one of all material desires.

One cannot purify one's heart by atonement alone. A patient suffering from syphilis goes to the doctor, who gives him an injection and charges a high fee. Yes, he may be cured, but when he again engages in illicit sex, he once again contracts syphilis. So his heart was not purified of the desire for illicit sex. But if one takes to Kṛṣṇa consciousness, he forgets illicit sex. That is the test of one's Kṛṣṇa consciousness. A sincere devotee never commits sin, because his heart has become purified by chanting the holy name and engaging in devotional service.

Of course, there are pseudo devotees who commit sinful activities on the strength of chanting Hare Kṛṣṇa. They are great offenders against the holy name. We should not use the holy name like a machine, thinking that because the chanting process consumes sinful reactions we can freely commit more sin. This is the greatest offense against the holy name of Kṛṣṇa. Whatever sins we may have previously committed are immediately eradicated by offenseless chanting of the holy name of the Lord, even just once. But we must not sin again. Lord Caitanya Mahāprabhu forgave the sinful Jagāi and Mādhāi, who had been drunkards, woman-hunters, meat-eaters, and gamblers. But these two sinners fell down at the lotus feet of Lord Caitanya and Nityānanda Prabhu and cried, "Sirs! We are so sinful! Kindly deliver us." Lord Caitanya agreed on the condition that they promise not to commit any more sins. He said, "Whatever you have done I shall excuse, but do not do it again." Thus Jagāi and Mādhāi vowed, "This is the end of our sinful activities. We shall not do them anymore." When a person is initiated by a spiritual master, the reactions of his sins immediately become nullified. But that does not mean he can again commit sins.

Kṛṣṇa consciousness means following in the footsteps of Lord Caitanya, and so we initiate disciples according to the principle he showed in the case of Jagāi and Mādhāi. We accept many people into our Society as duly initiated disciples, but only if they vow to observe these regulations: no more illicit sex, no more gambling, no more intoxication, and no more animal-killing or meat-eating. These regulations are necessary, because if one takes up spiritual life and at the same time goes on committing sinful activities, he will never be able to make progress. As Kṛṣṇa clearly says in the *Bhagavad-gītā* (7.28),

yeṣām tv anta-gataṁ pāpaṁ
janānāṁ puṇya-karmaṇām
te dvandva-moha-nirmuktā
bhajante māṁ dṛḍha-vratāḥ

"Persons who have acted piously in previous lives and in this life and whose sinful actions are completely eradicated are freed from the dualities of delusion, and they engage themselves in My service with determination."

If we are actually serious about entering into the kingdom of God, Vaikuṇṭha, then we should be very careful to follow the four regulative principles mentioned above. One must not have any sex except to have children within marriage. One must not indulge in intoxication. One must not gamble. And one must not eat meat, fish, or eggs or anything else beyond the foods established for human beings—grains, fruits, vegetables, milk, and sugar. Such foodstuffs are *sāttvika,* or pure and good, and they are allotted for human consumption. One should not imitate the cats and dogs, reasoning that because the animals are eating meat, human beings can do likewise. If everything eatable is food, why not eat stool? Stool is also food—hogs eat stool. But human beings should not eat like hogs, who will eat all kinds of unclean foods. We have to discriminate. If we want to enter into spiritual life, we must observe these four principles of restriction. This may mean undergoing some austerity, but this is the purpose of human life. When we have purified our existence through austerity, we will be eligible to enter into the kingdom of God, but without being purified, we can never enter.

Meditation on Kṛṣṇa's Form

If one chants the holy name of God—Hare Kṛṣṇa, Hare Kṛṣṇa, Kṛṣṇa Kṛṣṇa, Hare Hare/ Hare Rāma, Hare Rāma,

Rāma Rāma, Hare Hare—eventually he will see Kṛṣṇa's form, realize Kṛṣṇa's qualities, and remember Kṛṣṇa's pastimes. That is the effect of the pure chanting of the Hare Kṛṣṇa *mahā-mantra.*

Śrīla Viśvanātha Cakravartī Ṭhākura comments that the chanting of the holy name of the Lord has special significance that distinguishes it from the Vedic ritualistic ceremonies of atonement for severe, more severe, or most severe sins. There are twenty types of religious scriptures called *dharma-śāstras,* beginning with the *Manu-saṁhitā* and *Parāśara-saṁhitā,* but herein it is stressed that although one may become free from the reactions of the most sinful activities by following the religious principles of these scriptures, this cannot promote a sinful man to the stage of loving service to the Lord. On the other hand, chanting the holy name of the Lord even once not only frees one immediately from the reactions of the greatest sins, but also begins to raise one to the platform of rendering loving service to the Supreme Personality of Godhead. Thus one serves the Lord by remembering His form, attributes, and pastimes.

Śrīla Viśvanātha Cakravartī explains that it is because of the Lord's omnipotence that this is all possible simply by chanting His holy name. What cannot be achieved through the performance of Vedic rituals can easily be achieved through the chanting of the Lord's holy name. To chant the holy name and dance in ecstasy is so easy, sublime, and effective that one can readily achieve all the benefits of spiritual life simply by following this process. Therefore Śrī Caitanya Mahāprabhu declares, *paraṁ vijayate śrī-kṛṣṇa-saṅkīrtanam:* "All glories to the congregational chanting of Lord Kṛṣṇa's holy name!" The *saṅkīrtana* movement we have started offers the best process for immediately becoming purified of all sinful reactions and coming to the platform of spiritual life.

Although Ajāmila became fallen in his later days, in his youth he was a *brahmacārī* and was properly trained by his father. He knew the name, form, and pastimes of Nārāyaṇa, but by bad association he forgot them. However, as soon as he chanted the name of Lord Nārāyaṇa on his deathbed, he again remembered all his past pious activities, and therefore he was saved.

That chanting and hearing the Lord's name and glories is the best means of purifying the heart of sinful propensities is confirmed at the beginning of the *Śrīmad-Bhāgavatam* (1.2.17):

śṛṇvatāṁ sva-kathāḥ kṛṣṇah
puṇya-śravaṇa-kīrtanaḥ
hṛdy antaḥ stho hy abhadrāṇi
vidhunoti suhṛt satām

"Śrī Kṛṣṇa, the Personality of Godhead, who is the Supersoul in everyone's heart and the benefactor of the truthful devotee, cleanses desire for material enjoyment from the heart of the devotee who relishes His messages, which are in themselves virtuous when properly heard and chanted."

It is the special mercy of the Supreme Lord that as soon as He sees a person glorifying His name, form, and pastimes, He personally cleanses the dirt from that person's heart. Even if one does not understand the meaning of the Lord's name, form, and pastimes, one is purified simply by hearing or chanting them.

One's main purpose in human life should be to purify one's existence and achieve liberation. As long as one has a material body, one is understood to be impure. In such an impure, material condition, one cannot enjoy a truly blissful life, although everyone seeks it. Therefore everyone requires purification. As Lord Ṛṣabhadeva says in the *Śrīmad-Bhāgavatam* (5.5.1), *tapo divyaṁ putrakā yena sattvaṁ śuddhyed yasmād brahma-saukhyaṁ tv anantam:* "My dear sons, you must perform *tapasya*, austerity, to purify your existence; then you will come to the spiritual platform and enjoy unending spiritual happiness." The *tapasya* of chanting and glorifying the name, form, and pastimes of the Lord is a very easy purifying process by which everyone can become happy. Therefore everyone who desires the ultimate cleansing of his heart must adopt this process. Other processes, such as *karma, jñāna,* and *yoga,* cannot cleanse the heart absolutely.

Māyāvādīs, or impersonalists, cannot glorify the name, form, and pastimes of the Lord because they think that God has no form and that His pastimes are *māyā,* illusory. Why should God not have a form? We have a form because our father has a form. So why should the supreme father not have a form? In the *Bhagavad-gītā* (14.4) Kṛṣṇa says, *ahaṁ bīja-pradaḥ pitā:* "I am the seed-giving father of all beings." The Christians also believe that God is the supreme father. If the sons all have forms, how is it that the father has no form? We cannot be born of a father who is formless. *Īśvaraḥ paramaḥ kṛṣṇaḥ sac-cid-ānanda-vigrahaḥ:* "Kṛṣṇa is the supreme controller and the cause of all causes, and He possesses an eternal form of knowledge and bliss." (*Brahma-saṁhitā* 5.1) *Vigraha* means "form." If God is the cause of all causes, the creator, and He is creating all these forms, how can He be formless?

God has a form, but it is not a form like ours. His form is *sac-cid-ānanda,* but ours is just the opposite. God's form is *sat,* eternally existing, while man's form is *asat,* temporary. God's form is *cit,* full of knowledge, but ours is *acit,* full of ignorance. And His form is full of *ānanda,* bliss, but ours is full of *nirānanda,* misery. It is only because we cannot conceive of a form so different from ours that sometimes it is said God is *nirākāra,* without form.

God's form is transcendental. That means His body is not material but spiritual. His form is of a different nature than that to which we are accustomed. In the *Vedas* it is said that God sees but that He has no eyes. This means that God's eyes are unlike ours—they are spiritual, not material. We can see only so far, whereas God can see everything because He has eyes everywhere. His eyes, His form, His hands and legs are of a different nature than ours.

Unlike our knowledge, Kṛṣṇa's knowledge is unlimited. As He says in the *Bhagavad-gītā* (7.26), "I know past, present, future—everything." Earlier (*Bhagavad-gītā* 4.5) He reminds Arjuna, "Both you and I have taken many births. I remember them all, but you have forgotten them." Thus there is no limit to His knowledge. His knowledge, His body, and His happiness are completely different from our knowledge, body, and happiness. Therefore it is only out of ignorance that some people say the Absolute Truth is *nirākāra,* formless.

Thinking that God has no form is just imagination. It is material thought. We have a form, so He must have a form, though not a form like ours. Only fools think God is ultimately formless. Kṛṣṇa declares this in the *Bhagavad-gītā* (7.24): *avyaktaṁ vyaktim āpannaṁ manyante mām abuddhayaḥ.* "Unintelligent men think that I was impersonal before and have now assumed this personality." In another place in the *Bhagavad-gītā,* those who deride the personal form of God are called *mūḍhās,* or asses. God certainly has a form, but His form is entirely different from ours. That is the real understanding of *nirākāra.*

And just as Kṛṣṇa's form is not like our material forms, so His pastimes are also not of this material nature. Anyone who knows this is immediately liberated. Kṛṣṇa confirms this in the *Bhagavad-gītā* (4.9),

janma karma ca me divyam
evaṁ yo vetti tattvataḥ
tyaktvā dehaṁ punar janma
naiti mām eti so 'rjuna

"One who knows the transcendental nature of My appearance and activities does not, upon leaving the body, take his birth again in this material world, but attains my eternal abode." Simply by chanting the holy name of Kṛṣṇa purely, one can come to understand the pastimes of the Supreme Lord and thus become liberated. Chanting is easy and sublime. One who offenselessly chants Hare Kṛṣṇa will always remember Kṛṣṇa's form, pastimes, qualities, and entourage, and that remembrance will liberate him from all sinful reactions and all material bondage.

The Viṣṇudūtas here declare that although there are many methods prescribed in the *Vedas* for attaining liberation from sinful reactions, these methods are all insufficient, because they cannot elevate a person to the standard of absolute purity. Those who practice other methods of purification mentioned in the *Vedas* generally desire some material benefit, such as elevation to the heavenly kingdom. But a devotee does not care for elevation to the heavenly planets. A devotee doesn't care a fig for any planet in this material world, because he knows that the benefit of entering into the heavenly kingdom is temporary. We may live for thousands of years on a higher planet and enjoy a very high standard of life, complete with beautiful wife, abundant wealth, and the finest wine, but there is no permanent benefit. For a devotee, such a life is hellish, because he does not wish to live without Kṛṣṇa. That is genuine spiritual realization.

We simply care for Kṛṣṇa and how Kṛṣṇa will be happy. That is real happiness. We try to please Kṛṣṇa. Kaṁsa was also Kṛṣṇa conscious, insofar as he was always thinking of Kṛṣṇa, but his meditation was unfavorable. His meditation was on how to kill Kṛṣṇa. He was thinking of Kṛṣṇa, but he thought of Him as his enemy. That is certainly not *bhakti,* or devotion. Thinking of Kṛṣṇa but being opposed to His desire, opposed to satisfying Him, is not *bhakti.* One must act favorably in Kṛṣṇa consciousness. Arjuna was a devotee because he acted favorably, for the satisfaction of Kṛṣṇa. Materially speaking, Arjuna's actions appear unfavorable, but they were favorable as far as Kṛṣṇa was concerned. Therefore they were perfect and free from all sin.

Lord Kṛṣṇa's Transcendental Pastimes

It is important to understand the difference between activities of *bhakti* and ordinary pious activities. Cultivation of knowledge and pious activities is on the material platform. Piety does not amount to liberation. A pious man is situated on the platform of goodness, but he remains a conditioned soul, bound up by good reactions. One may even become a *brāhmaṇa,* a very pious man, but that does not mean he has become a devotee. And sometimes a devotee appears to act against the rules of mundane piety. Arjuna, for example, was an exalted devotee of Lord Kṛṣṇa, but he killed his relatives. Ignorant people may say, "Arjuna is not a good man. Look, he killed his grandfather, his teacher, and his nephews, devastating the entire family." But in the *Bhagavad-gītā* (4.3) Kṛṣṇa says to Arjuna, *bhakto 'si me:* "You are My very dear friend." In the estimation of the material world Arjuna may not be a good man, but because he is a soul surrendered to the desire of the Supreme Lord, he must be accepted as a devotee. While it is true that Arjuna killed his own kinsmen, in the eyes of Kṛṣṇa he remained a dear friend and devotee. That is the difference between a devotee and a good man of this world: A good man of this world tries to always act piously, for he knows that if he acts badly he will suffer sinful reactions; but a devotee, although naturally a very good man, can act like a bad man on Kṛṣṇa's order and still not fall down: he remains a pure devotee and is very dear to the Lord.

As mentioned above, hearing Kṛṣṇa's pastimes is very purifying, but such hearing has to be done with the right attitude. Some persons with material vision are very much attracted to Kṛṣṇa's *rāsa-līlā*—His pastimes with His cowherd girlfriends—but they do not appreciate His fighting and killing the demons. They do not know that the Absolute Truth, Kṛṣṇa, is good in any and all circumstances. Whether He is enjoying in the company of His devotees or killing the demons, He remains the Absolute Truth, and therefore all His pastimes are equally purifying to hear.

Generally people go to hear the *Śrīmad-Bhāgavatam* from professional reciters, who are especially fond of describing the *rāsa-līlā.* The people think, "Oh, Kṛṣṇa is embracing a girl—this is very nice." At times ten thousand people will gather to hear the *rāsa-līlā,* and in this way the reciters earn a nice profit. Thus people come to think that the *Śrīmad-Bhāgavatam* means the Tenth Canto, which contains the *rāsa-līlā* and other pastimes, but what they don't realize is that there are so many important instructions in the other cantos as well. Lord Kṛṣṇa, the summum bonum, is described in the Tenth Canto, and the other nine cantos are especially meant for purifying the heart so that one may understand Kṛṣṇa.

Therefore we instruct everyone first of all to read the first nine cantos of the *Śrīmad-Bhāgavatam* very carefully. Then one may read the Tenth Canto with proper understanding. Those who hear about Kṛṣṇa's *rāsa-līlā* and take it as an ordinary story cannot know Kṛṣṇa in truth. The *rāsa-līlā* is not an affair of lust. It is a transcendental pastime of love between Rādhā and Kṛṣṇa. According to Caitanya Mahāprabhu, the chapters of the *Śrīmad-Bhāgavatam* describing the *rāsa-līlā* are not meant for ordinary persons; they are meant for liberated persons only. Therefore these descriptions of the *rāsa-līlā* should not be described to ordinary people. Those who are advanced devotees, liberated from material contamination, can try to understand Kṛṣṇa's *rāsa-līlā.* One must not try to imagine the *rāsa-līlā* of Rādhā and Kṛṣṇa in mundane terms.

But even though ordinary hearers of *Śrīmad-Bhāgavatam* do not know the deep significance of Kṛṣṇa's *rāsa-līlā,* because they hear about Kṛṣṇa's pastimes they become purified. And if they hear from authorized sources, they will be promoted to the transcendental devotional platform. The disease within the heart is lust, the desire to enjoy, and by hearing from authorized sources about Kṛṣṇa's pastimes of loving exchanges with the *gopīs,* the deep-rooted lusty desires in the heart will be completely eradicated.

Unfortunately, most people do not hear the *Śrīmad-Bhāgavatam* from authoritative sources. They hear only from professional reciters. Therefore they remain materially diseased, full of lusty desires. Some become *sahajiyā*, pretending to be Kṛṣṇa and Rādhārāṇī and Her *gopī* friends. In this way they behave as if they were the supreme enjoyer.

The pure devotee's business is to satisfy Kṛṣṇa, and as soon as he chants the Hare Kṛṣṇa *mahā-mantra*, he remembers how to do so. In the material world, the living entities are inclined to go astray. The mind and senses generally become attracted to material objects of desire. But one should draw one's mind to the eternal by the practice of *bhakti-yoga*. Otherwise, one's mind and senses will force one to perform *karma*, activities for personal sense gratification. And as soon as a person engages in sense gratification, he commits sin. Therefore to avoid karmic activities, which quickly entangle one in the process of repeated birth and death, one must take to the process of Kṛṣṇa consciousness.

Here the Viṣṇudūtas advise us in the same way: If we want to be freed from the reactions of *karma*, we should glorify the Supreme Lord twenty-four hours a day. That will purify us. Śrīla Śrīdhara Svāmī says, "Instead of taking to prescribed ritualistic ceremonies, simply engage your mind in describing or glorifying the Supreme Personality of Godhead." This is the process of Kṛṣṇa consciousness.

In Kṛṣṇa consciousness, or devotional service, there are nine processes: hearing about the transcendental name, form, qualities, and pastimes of the Lord, chanting about these, remembering these, serving the lotus feet of the Lord, offering Him respectful worship, offering Him prayers, becoming His servant, considering Him one's friend, and surrendering everything to Him. One who practices one or more of these processes of devotional service throughout his life is sure to remember Kṛṣṇa at the time of death. That is the art of Kṛṣṇa consciousness. We cannot abandon all activities and simply chant Hare Kṛṣṇa; therefore we keep ourselves constantly engaged in practical devotional service so that our mind is fixed upon Kṛṣṇa. Then, at the time of death, we are sure to attain

His Divine Grace
A. C. Bhaktivedanta Swami Prabhupāda
Founder-Ācārya of the International Society for Krishna Consciousness

PLATE ONE: Lord Caitanya and His associates propagate the congrega
tional chanting of the Lord's holy names, the easiest means of self-realiza
tion for the modern age. *From left:* Śrī Advaitācārya, Lord Nityānanda
Lord Caitanya, Śrī Gadādhara, and Śrīvāsa Ṭhākura. (*p. 6*)

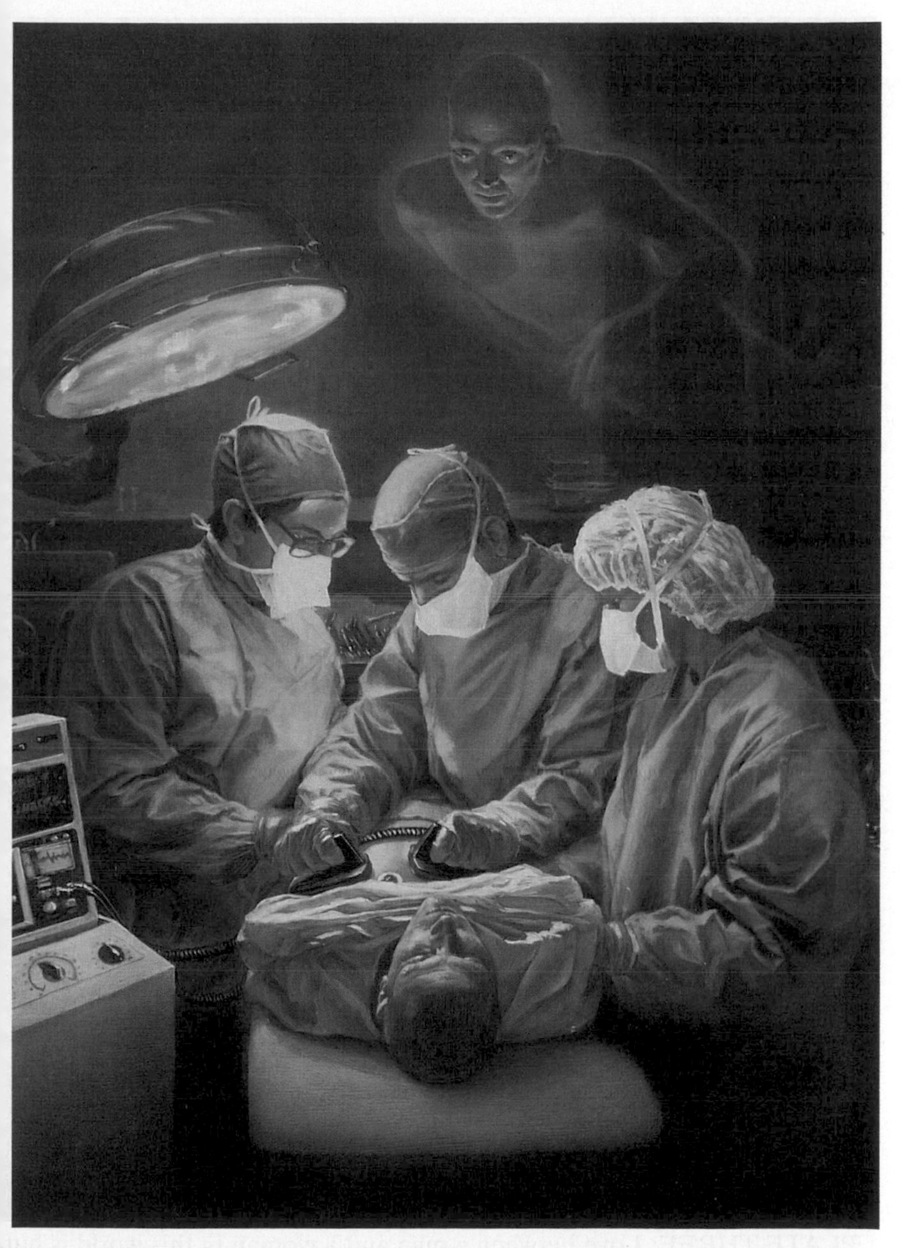

ATE TWO: Evidence shows that cardiac-arrest patients may undergo out-
-body experiences in which they observe their own resuscitation. (*p. viii*)

PLATE THREE: Love between a man and a woman in this world is but perverted reflection of the pure and perfect love between Lord Kṛṣṇa, th Absolute Truth, and His eternal consort, Śrīmatī Rādhārāṇī. (*p. 9*)

PLATE FOUR: In the heart of every living being resides an expansion of God called the Supersoul, who witnesses all our activities, sinful and pious. (*p. 44*)

PLATE FIVE: While in the forest on a mission for his father, the *brāhmaṇa* Ajāmila came upon a drunken, low-class man shamelessly embracing a prostitute. (*p. 69*)

PLATE SIX: After death, those who have transgressed the laws of God are taken to the court of Yamarāja, where he judges them and assigns them suitable hellish punishment. (*p. 151*)

PLATE SEVEN: Now pure and fully Kṛṣṇa conscious, Ajāmila boarded a spiritual airplane that would take him back to the kingdom of God. (*p. 140*)

total liberation from material existence.

One who is not practiced in devotional service cannot all of a sudden chant the holy name of Nārāyaṇa at the time of death. He must have prior practice in order to chant effectively. Therefore Caitanya Mahāprabhu has recommended, *kīrtanīyaḥ sadā hariḥ:* "One should chant the holy name of the Lord constantly." This is the best way of remembering Kṛṣṇa in this age, and always remembering Kṛṣṇa ensures our return home, back to Godhead. As the Lord promises in the *Bhagavad-gītā* (8.8),

abhyāsa-yoga-yuktena
cetasā nānya-gāminā
paramaṁ puruṣaṁ divyaṁ
yāti pārthānucintayan

"He who meditates on Me as the Supreme Personality of Godhead, his mind constantly engaged in remembering Me, undeviated from the path, is sure to reach Me."

That Ajāmila remembered Kṛṣṇa was not accidental. He had chanted the name of Lord Nārāyaṇa earlier in his life, but he forgot the Lord due to bad association. Nevertheless, the transcendental effect of his earlier practice was there at the time of his death, even though he was calling out the name of his youngest son, not intending to call for Kṛṣṇa.

Indiscriminate Mercy

As stated in the *Bhagavad-gītā* (8.6):

yaṁ yaṁ vāpi smaran bhāvaṁ
tyajaty ante kalevaram
taṁ tam evaiti kaunteya
sadā tad-bhāva-bhāvitaḥ

"Whatever state of being one remembers when he quits his body, that state he will attain without fail."

One who practices chanting the Hare Kṛṣṇa *mantra* is naturally expected to chant Hare Kṛṣṇa when he meets with some accident. Even without such practice, however, if one somehow or other chants the holy name of the Lord when he meets with an accident and dies, he will be saved from hellish life after death. For example, if a person falls from a high rooftop but somehow or other cries out "Hare Kṛṣṇa!" that cry will be heard by the Lord. Or, if in our sleep we dream that a tiger is coming to eat us and we chant Hare Kṛṣṇa in our sleep, the Lord hears that also.

Although Ajāmila indirectly chanted the holy name of Lord Nārāyaṇa through the medium of the name of his youngest son, he at once remembered Lord Nārāyaṇa. Therefore in Vedic society children are given God's names. It is not that the child becomes God. If we name a child Nārāyaṇa, it is understood that he is Nārāyaṇa dāsa, the servant of Lord Nārāyaṇa. Similarly, we give our disciples spiritual names, such as Viṣṇu dāsa, Vāmana dāsa, or Kṛṣṇa dāsa. That Ajāmila remembered Lord Nārāyaṇa by calling his son of the same name is confirmed in the *Śrīmad-Bhāgavatam*, which says that the power of the sound vibration of the holy name is absolute.

One attains freedom from all sinful reactions immediately upon recitation of the holy name, even if one does not understand the potency of the name. Whether one is chanting with devotion and reverence or without any faith, more sinful reactions are vanquished than a sinful man can commit. Kṛṣṇa's name has such unlimited potency. When Caitanya Mahāprabhu was chanting the Hare Kṛṣṇa *mahā-mantra* in Navadvīpa, the people used to imitate the Lord and His associates. At that time the land was ruled by Mohammedans, and sometimes the people would go to one of the government officials and complain, "The Hindus are chanting 'Hare Kṛṣṇa! Hare Kṛṣṇa!' dancing wildly, and thrashing their arms about." In this way they imitated the *saṅkīrtana* of Lord Caitanya. In Western countries the onlookers also imitate our chanting of Hare Kṛṣṇa when we go out to chant on the street. Even by imitating, however, they become purified. The holy name is so powerful that if someone derides us, saying, "Why are you chanting Hare Kṛṣṇa—it is nonsense!" he also gets spiritual benefit.

The chanting of Kṛṣṇa's holy name is like the sun rising in one's darkened heart. This universe is full of darkness, and only by Kṛṣṇa's arrangement for sunshine do we see light. As soon as the sun sets, the world comes under the influence of darkness. Likewise, our heart is full of the darkness of ignorance, but there is a light to dispel the darkness, and that light is Kṛṣṇa consciousness. Due to impious activities we are in ignorance, but to those who constantly engage in the service of the Lord with love and affection, Kṛṣṇa reveals Himself in the heart. By Kṛṣṇa's special mercy, the devotees are always kept in the light of Kṛṣṇa consciousness. Kṛṣṇa knows everyone's intention or motive, and His mercy is especially meant for those who are sincerely engaged in His service.

Kṛṣṇa is equal to everyone, and as such, His mercy is unlimited. However, He is very much inclined toward His devotees. If one is prepared to accept His mercy unlimitedly, then He is prepared to give it unlimitedly. On account of our envious nature, however, we are not prepared to take His mercy. In the *Bhagavad-gītā* (18.66) Kṛṣṇa says, *sarva-dharmān parityajya mām ekaṁ śaraṇaṁ vraja/ ahaṁ tvāṁ sarva-pāpebhyo mokṣayiṣyāmi:* "Just give up all other so-called religions and surrender to Me alone. I shall protect you from all sinful reactions." He openly offers His protection, but we do not take it. Sunlight is also equally distributed throughout the universe, but if we close the door and do not come out to take advantage of it, that is our own fault. Sunlight and moonlight do not discriminate, illuminating the houses of *brāhmaṇas* while leaving *caṇḍālas'* [dog-eaters'] houses in darkness. No, the light is distributed indiscriminately. Similarly, the mercy of Kṛṣṇa is equally available to everyone, but it is up to each individual to accept God's freely distributed mercy.

Naturally Kṛṣṇa bestows more mercy upon His devotee, because the devotee has the capacity to accept that mercy through service. The process of receiving the causeless mercy of the Lord is to render more and more service. We should be very enthusiastic to render service to the Lord. That enthusiasm will come when we chant Hare Kṛṣṇa with faith and determination.

Someone may argue, "I can see how chanting the holy name with faith is purifying, but if a man has no faith, then how will the holy name act?" Here are some examples: If an innocent child touches fire, knowingly or unknowingly, it will burn him. Or, if we give medicine to a child, it acts, even though he does not know the potency of the medicine or how it is acting. Poison also acts in this way. Similarly, the Hare Kṛṣṇa *mantra* acts, even though we may not know how or why. Even ignorant lower creatures are benefited when we chant loudly. This is confirmed by Śrīla Haridāsa Ṭhākura: "When one chants Hare Kṛṣṇa loudly, every living entity, moving or nonmoving, benefits." (*Caitanya-caritāmṛta, Antya-līlā* 3.69)

The potency of the chanting of Hare Kṛṣṇa is confirmed by the spread of the Kṛṣṇa consciousness movement. In countries where the Hare Kṛṣṇa movement is spreading, learned scholars and other thoughtful men are realizing its effectiveness. For example, Dr. J. Stillson Judah, a learned scholar, has been very much attracted to this movement because he has actually seen that it is turning hippies addicted to drugs into pure Vaiṣṇavas who voluntarily become servants of Kṛṣṇa and humanity. Even a few years ago, such hippies did not know the Hare Kṛṣṇa *mantra*, but now they are chanting it and becoming pure Vaiṣṇavas. Thus they are becoming free from all sinful activities, such as illicit sex, intoxication, meat-eating, and gambling. This is practical proof of the effectiveness of the Hare Kṛṣṇa *mantra*. One may or may not know the value of chanting the Hare Kṛṣṇa *mantra*, but if one somehow or other chants it, he will immediately be purified, just as one who takes a potent medicine will feel its effects, regardless of whether he takes it knowingly or unknowingly.

Another analogy: fire will act, regardless of whether handled by an innocent child or by someone well aware of its power. If a field of dry grass is set afire, either by a man who knows the power of fire or by a child who does not, the grass will be burned to ashes. Similarly, a person may or may not know the power of chanting the Hare Kṛṣṇa *mantra*, but if he chants the holy name, he will become free from all sinful reactions. This is the correct conclusion of the Viṣṇudūtas.

Extended Lease on Life

The servants of Yamarāja are so powerful that generally they cannot be hindered anywhere, but this time they were baffled and disappointed in their attempt to take away a man they considered sinful. Therefore they immediately returned to Yamarāja and described to him everything that had happened. They thought that it was unnatural that Ajāmila, who had seemed eligible to be brought before Yamarāja, had been released by the Viṣṇudūtas.

Now Ajāmila was fully Kṛṣṇa conscious. By the divine association of the Viṣṇudūtas, who were highly elevated Vaiṣṇavas, Ajāmila came to his full consciousness. He had been arrested, but then he had been released, and now he was free from all fear. This is liberation. When one is situated in Kṛṣṇa consciousness by the association of Vaiṣṇavas, or devotees of the Lord, one becomes free from all fear. This position is eternal. Ajāmila became fearless due to being reinstated in his constitutional position. At once he began to offer nice prayers to the Viṣṇudūtas: *vāñchā-kalpatarubhyaś ca kṛpā-sindhubhya eva ca:* "I offer my respectful obeisances unto the devotees of the Lord, who are just like desire trees and oceans of mercy." This is the life of a devotee: he is always offering prayers to other devotees. First he offers respects to his spiritual master, next to his grand–spiritual master, next to his great-grand–spiritual master, and then to all devotees of Lord Kṛṣṇa.

Vaiṣṇavas are also Viṣṇudūtas because they carry out the

orders of Kṛṣṇa. Lord Kṛṣṇa is very eager for all the conditioned souls rotting in this material world to surrender to Him and be saved from material pangs in this life and punishment in hellish conditions after death. A Vaiṣṇava therefore tries to bring conditioned souls to their senses. Those who are fortunate like Ajāmila are saved by the Viṣṇudūtas, or Vaiṣṇavas, and thus they return home, back to Godhead.

Good examples of merciful Vaiṣṇavas are the six Gosvāmīs. They scrutinizingly studied all kinds of scriptures to establish the principles of Kṛṣṇa consciousness. In the *Bhakti-rasāmṛta-sindhu* (*The Nectar of Devotion*) Śrīla Rūpa Gosvāmī quotes many verses from different scriptures in support of the principles of *bhakti.* Why did he and the other Gosvāmīs go to so much trouble and research? It is very laborious to research the Vedic literature in search of authoritative statements, and then to assimilate them in order to support the Vedic conclusions. But the six Gosvāmīs took up that laborious work out of compassion for humanity.

Spreading Kṛṣṇa consciousness, as the six Gosvāmīs did, is the best welfare work for all humanity. There seem to be many other welfare activities, but their benefit is only temporary. The great welfare work of spreading Kṛṣṇa consciousness, undertaken by exalted personalities such as the six Gosvāmīs of Vṛndāvana, has real value for all men because it is based upon substantial spiritual truth. The Vaiṣṇavas are just like desire trees (*kalpa-vṛkṣa*), for they can fulfill all one's spiritual desires. And thus they are also oceans of mercy (*kṛpā-sindhu*).

Ajāmila heard the conversation between the Yamadūtas and the Viṣṇudūtas, and simply by hearing he was completely cleansed of all material contamination. Such is the purifying effect of hearing about Kṛṣṇa. Anyone who regularly hears the *Śrīmad-Bhāgavatam,* the *Bhagavad-gītā,* the *Caitanya-caritāmṛta,* the *Bhakti-rasāmṛta-sindhu,* or any other Vaiṣṇava literature gets the same benefit as Ajāmila and becomes free of all material contamination.

Ajāmila was very grateful to the Viṣṇudūtas, and he immediately offered his respects by bowing down before them. Similarly, we have to make firm our relationships with the servants of Lord Viṣṇu. As Caitanya Mahāprabhu has said, *gopī-bhartuḥ pada-kamalayor dāsa-dāsānudāsaḥ:* "One should consider oneself the servant of the servant of the servant of Kṛṣṇa." Without offering respects to the servant of Kṛṣṇa, no one can approach Kṛṣṇa.

After Ajamila had offered his respects to the Viṣṇudūtas, he prepared to say something out of gratitude. But they immediately took their leave because they preferred that he glorify the Supreme Lord instead. Since all his sinful reactions had been vanquished, Ajāmila was now prepared to glorify the Lord. Indeed, one cannot glorify the Lord sincerely unless one is free from all sinful activities. This is confirmed by Kṛṣṇa Himself in the *Bhagavad-gītā* (7.28):

yeṣāṁ tv anta-gataṁ pāpaṁ
janānaṁ puṇya-karmaṇām
te dvanda-moha-nirmuktā
bhajante māṁ dṛḍha-vratāḥ

"Persons who have acted piously in previous lives and in this life and whose sinful actions are completely eradicated are freed from the duality of delusion, and they engage themselves in My service with determination." The Viṣṇudūtas made Ajāmila aware of devotional service so that He might soon become fit to return home, back to Godhead. To increase his eagerness to glorify the Lord, they disappeared so that he would feel separation in their absence. In the mood of separation, glorification of the Lord is very intense.

3

AJĀMILA REPENTS

CHAPTER

The Moment of Truth

Śukadeva Gosvāmī continued: By hearing the discourses between the Yamadūtas and the Viṣṇudūtas, Ajāmila could understand the religious principles that act under the three modes of material nature. These principles are mentioned in the three *Vedas*. He could also understand the transcendental religious principles, which are above the modes of material nature and which concern the relationship between the living being and the Supreme Personality of Godhead. Furthermore, Ajāmila heard glorification of the name, fame, qualities, and pastimes of the Supreme Personality of Godhead. He thus became a perfectly pure devotee. He could then remember his past sinful activities, which he greatly regretted having performed.

Ajāmila said: "Alas, being a servant of my senses, how degraded I became! I fell down from my position as a duly qualified *brāhmaṇa* and begot children in the womb of a prostitute. Alas, all condemnation upon me! I acted so sinfully that I degraded my family tradition. Indeed, I gave up my chaste and beautiful young wife to have sexual intercourse with a fallen prostitute accustomed to drinking wine. All condemnation upon me! My father and mother were old and had no one to look after them. Because I did not take care of them, they lived with great difficulty. Alas, like an abominable lower-class man, I ungratefully left them in that condition.

"It is now clear that as a consequence of such activities, a sinful person like me must be thrown into hellish conditions meant for those who have broken religious principles

CHAPTER 17

The Moment of Truth

Śukadeva Gosvāmī continued: After hearing the discourses between the Yamadūtas and the Viṣṇudūtas, Ajāmila could understand the religious principles that act under the three modes of materal nature. These principles are mentioned in the three *Vedas*. He could also understand the transcendental religious principles, which are above the modes of material nature and which concern the relationship between the living being and the Supreme Personality of Godhead. Furthermore, Ajāmila heard glorification of the name, fame, qualities, and pastimes of the Supreme Personality of Godhead. He thus became a perfectly pure devotee. He could then remember his past sinful activities, which he greatly regretted having performed.

Ajāmila said, "Alas, being a servant of my senses, how degraded I became! I fell down from my position as a duly qualified *brāhmaṇa* and begot children in the womb of a prostitute. Alas, all condemnation upon me! I acted so sinfully that I degraded my family tradition. Indeed, I gave up my chaste and beautiful young wife to have sexual intercourse with a fallen prostitute accustomed to drinking wine. All condemnation upon me! My father and mother were old and had no one to look after them. Because I did not take care of them, they lived with great difficulty. Alas, like an abominable lower-class man, I ungratefully left them in that condition.

"It is now clear that as a consequence of such activities, a sinful person like me must be thrown into hellish conditions meant for those who have broken religious principles

and must there suffer extreme miseries.

"Was this a dream I saw, or was it reality? I saw fearsome men with ropes in their hands coming to arrest me and drag me away. Where have they gone? And where have those four liberated and very beautiful persons gone who released me from arrest and saved me from being dragged down to the hellish regions?

"I am certainly most abominable and unfortunate to have merged into the ocean of sinful activities. But nevertheless, because of my previous spiritual activities, I could see those four exalted personalities who came to rescue me. Now I feel exceedingly happy because of their visit.

"Were it not for my past devotional service, how could I, a most unclean keeper of a prostitute, have gotten an opportunity to chant the holy name of Nārāyaṇa when I was just ready to die? Certainly it would not have been possible." (*Śrīmad-Bhāgavatam* 6.2.24–33)

Repentance

Having heard the conversation between the Yamadūtas and the Viṣṇudūtas, Ajāmila became firmly fixed in Kṛṣṇa consciousness. He began to lament, "How unfortunate I was to engage in so many sinful activities!" This is the proper attitude for a Kṛṣṇa conscious devotee. Whatever he may have done in the past, no matter how sinful, when he comes in contact with devotees and hears transcendental topics in relation to the Supreme Personality of Godhead (*bhāgavata-kathā*), he becomes purified and laments his previous condition. Indeed, the symptom of his purification is that he laments having behaved so sinfully. He repents and discontinues his past grievous conduct.

Ajāmila was now at the stage of devotional service in which one is freed from all material impediments and is completely satisfied (*ahaituky apratihatā yayātmā suprasīdati*). Having reached this platform, Ajāmila began to lament for his past materialistic activities and glorify the name, fame, form, and pastimes of the Supreme Personality of Godhead.

One who takes to Kṛṣṇa consciousness naturally endeavors to follow the rules of devotional service, and he regularly chants the Hare Kṛṣṇa *mahā-mantra:* Hare Kṛṣṇa, Hare Kṛṣṇa, Kṛṣṇa Kṛṣṇa, Hare Hare/ Hare Rāma, Hare Rāma, Rāma Rāma, Hare Hare. A person should not suppose that because he has taken to Kṛṣṇa consciousness he can continue his sinful activities and have their effects counteracted. We have repeatedly warned that this is the greatest offense against the holy name. Like Ajāmila, one should repent, "How unfortunate I was to engage in so many sinful activities! But now, by the grace of Kṛṣṇa, I have come to know that I was acting improperly."

Thus Ajāmila greatly repented, remembering all his sinful activities. He remembered that he had been trained by his father to be a first-class *brāhmaṇa,* that he had been educated in the science of the *Vedas,* and that he had married a beautiful and chaste wife, a girl who was innocent and highly qualified, having come from a respectable *brāhmaṇa* family. Ajāmila now lamented, "I rejected her and accepted a prostitute, an abominable drunkard!"

It is a Vedic regulation that men of the higher classes—*brāhmaṇas, kṣatriyas,* and *vaiśyas*—do not beget children in the wombs of lower-class women. Therefore the custom in Vedic society is to examine the horoscopes of a girl and boy being considered for marriage to see whether their combination is suitable. Vedic astrology reveals whether one has been born in the *brāhmaṇa* class, the *kṣatriya* class, the *vaiśya* class, or the *śūdra* class, according to the three qualities of material nature. The horoscope must be examined because a marriage between a boy of the *brāhmaṇa* class and a girl of the *śūdra* class is incompatible; married life would be miserable for both husband and wife. Of course, this is a material calculation according to the three modes of nature, yet it is important for the peace and prosperity of the family and society. But if the boy and girl are devotees, there need be no such considerations. A devotee is transcendental, and therefore in a marriage between devotees, the boy and girl form a very happy combination.

Ajāmila thought, "Because I failed to be self-controlled, I was degraded to an abominable life and all my brahminical qualifications were nullified." This is the mentality of one who is becoming a pure devotee. When one is elevated to the platform of devotional service by the grace of the Lord and the spiritual master, one first regrets his past sinful activities. This helps one advance in spiritual life. The Viṣṇudūtas had given Ajāmila the chance to become a pure devotee, and the first duty of a devotee is to regret his past sinful activities in illicit sex, intoxication, meat-eating, and gambling. Not only should a devotee give up his past bad habits, but he must always regret his past sinful acts. This is the standard of pure devotion.

Debts to Pay

Ajāmila repented his negligence in performing his duty to his wife, father, and mother. It is the duty of grown-up children to render service to their aged parents. This practice should be reintroduced into present society. Otherwise, what is the use of family life? Proper family life means that the husband should be protective, the wife chaste, and the children grateful to their father and mother. Children should think, "My father and mother gave me so much service. When I was unable to walk, they carried me. When I was unable to eat, they fed me. They gave me an education. They gave me life." A bona fide son thinks of ways to render service to his father and mother. And just as a woman is expected to be faithful to her husband, so the husband should be grateful for her service and protect her. Because of his association with a prostitute, however, Ajāmila had abandoned all his duties. Regretting this, he now considered himself quite fallen.

According to the Vedic social system, as soon as one takes birth he becomes indebted to so many persons. We are indebted to the *ṛṣis,* or great sages, because we derive knowledge from their transcendental writings, such as the

Śrīmad-Bhāgavatam, compiled by Śrīla Vyāsadeva. The authors of the scripture know past, present, and future, and we are urged to take advantage of such invaluable knowledge. Thus we are indebted to the sages.

We are also indebted to the demigods, for they manage the affairs of the universe, supplying it with every essential—sunshine from the sun-god, Sūrya; moonshine from the moon-god, Candra; air from Vāyu; and so on. Each element is controlled by a particular demigod.

We are also indebted to ordinary living entities from whom we take service. For example, we take milk from the cow. According to Vedic understanding, the cow is considered one of our mothers because we drink her milk, just as at birth we drink our mother's milk. The *Śrīmad-Bhāgavatam* lists seven mothers: our own mother, the wife of our teacher or spiritual master, the wife of a *brāhmaṇa*, the wife of the king, the nurse, the cow, and the earth. We are indebted to all seven of these mothers, and also to our father, brothers, friends, relatives, and forefathers.

Also, if someone accepts charity, he becomes indebted, and that debt has to be repaid, just as borrowed money must be repaid. Therefore devotees should not accept charity from anyone unless they intend to spend it in Kṛṣṇa's service. For a devotee to accept donations just to satisfy his belly is a great sin. *Brāhmaṇas* and *sannyāsīs* who accept charity from others must accept it with great caution. According to the Vedic social structure, only the *brahmacārī*, *sannyāsī*, and *brāhmaṇa* are allowed to collect money in charity. An ordinary householder must not. The *brahmacārī* may collect alms from the public for serving his spiritual master, and a *sannyāsī* may collect money for serving God, Kṛṣṇa. The *Vedas* likewise direct people to give charity to the *brāhmaṇas* because they know how to spend it for Kṛṣṇa. Charity given to a worthy person is in the mode of goodness, charity given for one's own personal benefit is touched with the mode of passion, and charity given without any consideration is sunk in the mode of ignorance. For instance, if we give money to a rascal, he will likely take it to the nearest liquor shop. Those who are rich may think it does not matter—they can afford not to discriminate—but the scriptures describe these three kinds of charity.

We may well ask, How can one hope to liquidate all his debts? The answer is: only by taking shelter of the lotus feet of Kṛṣṇa, or Mukunda. The name Mukunda indicates one who liberates us from material contamination. We are indebted to the demigods, but we cannot take shelter of them. If we actually want shelter, we should take shelter of Kṛṣṇa, because He alone can free us from all debts. Kṛṣṇa is the Supreme Personality of Godhead, and if He excuses us, then all other departmental managers, such as the demigods, must also excuse us.

Ajāmila understood his position as a debtor, but since he had now taken shelter at the lotus feet of Mukunda, all his debts were cleared. Simply by taking shelter of Lord Nārāyaṇa, who is nondifferent from Mukunda, Ajāmila became free. Similarly, if we want to be free from all sinful reactions, we have no alternative but to surrender to Kṛṣṇa. As Kṛṣṇa recommends, *mām ekaṁ śaraṇaṁ vraja:* "Simply surrender unto Me." We should follow Kṛṣṇa's advice. Otherwise, it will be very difficult to liquidate all our debts to so many persons, especially in this Age of Kali.

Permanent Credit

In the material world there is danger at every step. Even for those who are pure devotees there is the danger of falling down from the standard of purity. However, in the *Śrīmad-Bhāgavatam* (1.5.17) Nārada Muni assures us,

tyaktvā sva-dharmaṁ caraṇāmbujaṁ harer
bhajann apakvo 'tha patet tato yadi
yatra kva vābhadram abhūd amuṣya kiṁ
ko vārtha āpto 'bhajatāṁ sva-dharmataḥ

The word *dharma* in this verse means "occupational duties." A *brāhmaṇa,* for example, has certain occupational duties. Similarly, a *kṣatriya* has his, and so also do the *vaiśya* and *śūdra.* If a person gives up his occupational duties and takes to Kṛṣṇa consciousness, strictly following all the rules and regulations, but if due to his immature execution of devotional service he falls down, there is still no loss for him. Whatever he does as service to the Supreme Lord, although it may be a small percentage of his whole life, will remain to his credit. He does not lose it.

On the other hand, one who perfectly executes his occupational duties but fails to worship Kṛṣṇa ultimately gains nothing. Strictly discharging one's occupational duties means living a life of piety. But suppose through these pious activities you are promoted to the heavenly kingdom. Kṛṣṇa explains in the *Bhagavad-gītā* that as soon as the effects of your pious activities are finished, you will be forced to return to this planet. Another point: If a person performs pious activities in this life, such as giving in charity, he must return here in the next life to accept the beneficial results of his pious actions. That means he must accept another term of material life. So it is not a sound idea to hope for acquisition of the effects of pious activities.

Unfortunately, even in India people are more inclined to perform pious activities, such as giving in charity, than to take up devotional service to Kṛṣṇa. They hope that by performing such *tapasya,* or austerity, they will be elevated at death to a higher standard of material life in the heavenly planets. They also worship demigods for this purpose, or to gain a benediction in this life. Lord Śiva, for example, very quickly gives his worshiper material benedictions—whatever his devotee wants. He is very kind. He is known as Āśutoṣa, "he who is easily satisfied." For this reason people are fond of worshiping him for material prosperity. But Śrī Kṛṣṇa condemns such worship in the *Bhagavad-gītā* (7.20): *kāmais tais tair hṛta-jñānāḥ prapadyante 'nya-devatāḥ.* "Those whose intelligence has been stolen by material desires surrender unto the demigods."

The *Śrīmad-Bhāgavatam* tells the story of Vṛkāsura, who

sought a terrible benediction from Lord Śiva. Vṛkāsura asked that whoever he would touch upon the head would be destroyed. This is the sort of benediction sought by demons. Rāvaṇa and Hiraṇyakaśipu also received such benedictions. They thought that by becoming powerful they could elude death. This is typical demoniac mentality.

None of these demons, however, was saved from death by the benediction received from the demigods. Rather, ultimately they were all killed by the Supreme Lord. It is nature's law that everyone here must die. No one who takes birth in the material world can live eternally. The material world is called Martyaloka, meaning that every living entity here is subject to birth, death, old age, and disease. In illusion, people do not see this. They try to adjust their material condition so that they can live perpetually. Modern scientists also aspire to be immortal, in imitation of Hiraṇyakaśipu. This is all foolishness. One should not be afraid of dying, but one should be cautious and ask, "What sort of situation will I attain in my next life as a result of my activities?"

A devotee is never afraid of death. He simply prays to Kṛṣṇa, "I may die and take birth again repeatedly, as You like. But I only ask that, in whatever condition I may live, by Your mercy I will never forget You." A devotee is not afraid, but he is cautious not to fall down. At the same time, he knows that whatever percentage of devotional service he renders is to his permanent credit. The story of Ajāmila is the perfect illustration of that point. We should follow the rules and regulations very strictly, but even if we fall down, there is no loss. That is the statement of Nārada Muni quoted above. Even if one takes to Kṛṣṇa consciousness on the basis of sentiment and executes devotional service for only some time and again returns to material life, whatever service he has rendered is recorded, and one day he will be saved, just as Ajāmila was saved.

After the Viṣṇudūtas disappeared, Ajāmila at first wondered whether he had been dreaming that they had come to release him from the binding ropes of the Yamadūtas. When Ajāmila was on his deathbed, practically in a coma, he actually saw the Yamadūtas and Viṣṇudūtas, but it seemed to him that he was just dreaming. When he saw that he was in fact released from the fearsome agents of Yamarāja, he wanted to see the Viṣṇudūtas again. They had appeared very splendid. Their bodily features were just like those of Lord Viṣṇu, and they were decorated like Him and carried the four symbols of His potency: the conchshell, lotus, club, and disc. Their bodies shone with a very beautiful luster, and their dress was of golden silk. Therefore Ajāmila inquired, "Where are those beautiful personalities who released me from the bondage of the Yamadūtas?"

Ajāmila thought, "My whole life was full of sinful activities, so how could I be worthy of seeing such great personalities?" He concluded, "Perhaps in my previous life I did something good, and as a result I have been allowed to see the Viṣṇudūtas." In fact, early in life Ajāmila had been a faithful servant of Lord Nārāyaṇa, and as a result he was able to see the Viṣṇudūtas. It was the good association Ajāmila had been blessed with in his early days that saved him. As stated in the *Caitanya-caritāmṛta* (*Madhya* 22.54),

> *'sādhu-saṅga', 'sādhu-saṅga'—sarva-śāstre kaya*
> *lava-mātra sādhu-saṅge sarva-siddhi haya*

"The verdict of all revealed scriptures is that by even a moment's association with a pure devotee, one can attain all success." In the beginning of his life Ajāmila was certainly very pure, and he associated with devotees and *brāhmaṇas;* because of that pious activity, even though he was fallen he was inspired to name his son Nārāyaṇa. Certainly this was due to good counsel given from within by the Supreme Personality of Godhead. As the Lord says in the *Bhagavad-gītā* (15.15), *sarvasya cāhaṁ hṛdi sanniviṣṭho mattaḥ smṛtir jñānam apohanaṁ ca:* "I am seated in everyone's heart, and from Me come remembrance, knowledge, and forgetfulness." The Lord is so kind that if one has ever rendered service to Him, the Lord never forgets him. Thus the Lord, from within, gave Ajāmila the inspiration to name his youngest son Nārāyaṇa so that in affection he would constantly call "Nārāyaṇa! Nārāyaṇa!" and thus be saved from the most fearful and dangerous condition at the time of his death. Such is the mercy of Kṛṣṇa. *Guru-kṛṣṇa-prasāde pāya bhakti-latā-bīja:* by the mercy of the *guru* and Kṛṣṇa, one receives the seed of *bhakti,* devotional service. Watering this seed by the process of hearing and chanting the name of the Lord saves a devotee from the greatest fear.

In our Kṛṣṇa consciousness movement we therefore change a devotee's name to one that reminds him of Viṣṇu. If at the time of death the devotee can remember his own name, such as Kṛṣṇa dāsa or Govinda dāsa, he can be saved from the greatest danger. Therefore the change of names at the time of initiation is essential. The Kṛṣṇa consciousness movement is so meticulous that it gives one a good opportunity to remember Kṛṣṇa somehow or other.

Remembrance of Kṛṣṇa at the time of death is generally possible only for persons who have established an intimate relationship with Kṛṣṇa throughout a lifetime of devotional service. When Ajāmila was a young boy he was trained by his father to be completely faithful to the Lord, and until the age of twenty he served Lord Nārāyaṇa very nicely. Although Ajāmila had fallen down from the standard of devotional service to Lord Nārāyaṇa and forgotten his relationship with Him, Nārāyaṇa did not forget, and in Ajāmila's hour of need He reciprocated His devotee's love. Thus Ajāmila was given the presence of mind to remember Nārāyaṇa at the time of death.

Kṛṣṇa is very appreciative of even a small amount of devotional service. He confirms this in the *Bhagavad-gītā* (2.40),

nehābhikrama-nāśo 'sti
pratyavāyo na vidyate

svalpam apy asya dharmasya
trāyate mahato bhayāt

"In this endeavor there is no loss or diminution, and a little advancement on this path protects one from the most fearful type of danger." If a person practices even a small amount of devotional service, it can save him from the greatest danger. So why not take to Kṛṣṇa consciousness? Engage in devotional service always, twenty-four hours a day. Then there is no question of danger. One who has become Kṛṣṇa conscious is fearless. He knows he is under the protection of Kṛṣṇa.

CHAPTER 18

Pilgrim with a Purpose

Ajāmila continued: "I am a shameless cheater who has killed his brahminical culture. Indeed, I am sin personified. What am I in comparison to the all-auspicious chanting of the holy name of Lord Nārāyaṇa?

"I am such a sinful person, but since I have now gotten this opportunity, I must completely control my mind, life, and senses and always engage in devotional service so that I may not fall again into the deep darkness and ignorance of material life.

"Because of identifying oneself with the body, one is subjected to desires for sense gratification, and thus one performs many kinds of pious and impious acts. This is what constitutes material bondage. Now I shall disentangle myself from my material bondage, which has been caused by the Supreme Lord's illusory energy in the form of a woman. Being a most fallen soul, I was vicitimized by the illusory energy and have become like a dancing dog led around by a woman's hand. Now I shall give up all lusty desires and free myself from this illusion. I shall become a merciful, well-wishing friend to all living entities and always absorb myself in Kṛṣṇa consciousness.

"Simply because I chanted the holy name of the Lord in the association of devotees, my heart is now becoming purified. Therefore I shall not fall victim again to the false lures of material sense gratification. Now that I have become fixed in the Absolute Truth, I shall no longer identify myself with the body. I shall give up the false conceptions of 'I' and 'mine' and fix my mind on the lotus feet of Kṛṣṇa."

Śukadeva Gosvāmī continued: Because of a moment's association with devotees—the Viṣṇudūtas—Ajāmila detached himself from the material conception of life with determination. Thus free from all material attraction, he immediately started for Hardwar. There he took shelter at a Viṣṇu temple, where he executed the process of *bhakti-yoga*. He controlled his senses and fully applied his mind in the service of the Lord. Thus Ajāmila fully engaged in devotional service, and in this way he detached his mind from the process of sense gratification and became fully absorbed in thinking of the form of the Lord.

When his intelligence and mind were fixed upon the form of the Lord, Ajāmila once again saw before him four celestial persons. He could understand that they were those he had seen previously, and thus he offered them his obeisances by bowing down before them.

Upon seeing the Viṣṇudūtas, Ajāmila gave up his material body at Hardwar on the bank of the Ganges. He regained his original, spiritual body—one appropriate for an associate of the Lord. Accompanied by the order-carriers of Lord Viṣṇu, he then boarded an airplane made of gold. Passing through the airways, he went directly to the abode of Lord Viṣṇu, the husband of the goddess of fortune.

Because of bad association, Ajāmila had given up all brahminical culture and religious principles. Becoming most fallen, he had stolen, drunk liquor, and performed other abominable acts. He had even kept a prostitute. Thus he had been destined to be carried away to hell by the order-carriers of Yamarāja. But he was immediately rescued simply by a glimpse of the chanting of the holy name Nārāyaṇa.

Therefore one who desires freedom from material bondage should adopt the process of chanting and glorifying the name, fame, form, and pastimes of the Supreme Personality of Godhead, at whose feet all the holy places

stand. One cannot derive this benefit from other methods, such as pious atonement, speculative knowledge, or meditation in mystic *yoga*, because even after following such methods a person will take to fruitive activities again, unable to control his mind, which is contaminated by the base qualities of nature, namely passion and ignorance.

Because this very confidential historical narration has the potency to vanquish all sinful reactions, a person who hears or describes it with faith and devotion is no longer doomed to hellish life, regardless of his having a material body and regardless of how sinful he may have been. Indeed, the Yamadūtas do not approach him even to see him. After giving up his body, he returns home, back to Godhead, where he is very respectfully received and worshiped.

While suffering at the time of death, Ajāmila chanted the holy name of the Lord, and although the chanting was directed toward his son, he nevertheless returned home, back to Godhead. Therefore if a person faithfully and inoffensively chants the holy name of the Lord, what doubt is there that he will return to Godhead? (*Śrīmad-Bhāgavatam* 6.2.34–49)

Determination

The holy name of God is all-auspicious. Therefore for one who constantly practices chanting Hare Kṛṣṇa, Hare Kṛṣṇa, Kṛṣṇa Kṛṣṇa, Hare Hare/ Hare Rāma, Hare Rāma, Rāma Rāma, Hare Hare, there cannot be any inauspiciousness. Just by chanting, one is put into an auspicious condition of life perpetually.

Those engaged in broadcasting the holy name through the Kṛṣṇa consciousness movement should always consider what their position was before they came and what it is now. They had fallen into abominable lives as meat-eaters, drunkards, and woman-hunters, performing all kinds of sinful activities, but now they have been given the opportunity to chant the Hare Kṛṣṇa *mantra*. Therefore they should always appreciate this opportunity. By the grace of the Lord we are opening many branches, and the members of this movement should use this good fortune to chant the holy name of the Lord and serve the Supreme Personality of Godhead directly. They must be conscious of the difference between their present conditoins and their past conditions and should always be very careful not to fall from the most exalted life of Kṛṣṇa consciousness. Every devotee of Kṛṣṇa should have this determination. Devotees have been elevated to an exalted position by the mercy of Kṛṣṇa and the spiritual master, and if they remember that this is a great opportunity and pray to Kṛṣṇa that they will not fall again, their lives will be successful.

Being fully Kṛṣṇa conscious, Ajāmila settled the debts he had accrued due to his sinful activities, and he was filled with determination to continue chanting the holy name of the Lord, Nārāyaṇa: "If I continue chanting the holy name of the Lord," he thought, "I will always be engaged in the highest welfare activities for the benefit of all living entities, and I shall be very peaceful." Because he was now purified of all sinful reactions, Ajāmila realized that Kṛṣṇa was dictating from within his heart that his duty was to become every living entity's well-wisher.

Everyone's Friend

The devotees of the Lord are very kind. They preach Kṛṣṇa consciousness for the welfare of the general public, and thus they are friends to all living entities. Others cannot be the well-wishers of all. The politicians, for example, engage in so-called service of their countrymen, but they are not the true friends of everyone in the land, because although they may serve the interests of their fellow men, they do not look after the interests of the animals. In this way they discriminate. A devotee is a friend to every living entity, whether man, animal, insect, or plant. A devotee is not willing to kill even an ant, but a nondevotee will mercilessly send animals to the slaughterhouse and in the same breath declare himself the friend of everyone.

Kṛṣṇa, God, is the best friend of every living entity. He is equal to everyone. He is not only the friend of the residents of Vṛndāvana—the *gopīs,* His parents, the cowherd men and boys, the cows—but He is everyone's friend, because everyone is part and parcel of Him. So Kṛṣṇa loves everyone unlimitedly. And Kṛṣṇa's devotees inherit the superexcellent loving qualities of Kṛṣṇa. Therefore they are truly the friends of everyone.

The *karmīs,* fruitive workers, perform sinful acts for their personal interest, killing innocent animals and becoming puffed up with their material opulence. *Jñānīs,* those in search of liberation through knowledge of Brahman, are also interested only in themselves. But *bhaktas,* or devotees, are interested in the well-being of everyone. A devotee is especially merciful to the fallen, conditioned souls. Lord Caitanya Mahāprabhu is the personification of *bhakti,* loving devotion to God, teaching all of us how to become devotees. He is therefore called *patita-pāvana,* or the one who delivers the fallen, conditioned souls. Anyone following in His footsteps is also *patita-pāvana.* Ajāmila was now in this same mood, and thus he thought, "Now I shall be able to become the friend of all living entities and become peaceful."

This should be the standard of determination for all Kṛṣṇa conscious persons. A devotee of Kṛṣṇa should free himself from the clutches of *māyā,* and he should also be compassionate to all others suffering in those clutches. The activities of the Kṛṣṇa consciousness movement are meant not only for oneself but for others also. This is the perfection of Kṛṣṇa consciousness. One who is interested only in his own salvation is not as advanced in Kṛṣṇa consciousness as one who feels compassion for others and who therefore propagates Kṛṣṇa consciousness. Such an advanced devotee will never fall down, for Kṛṣṇa will give him special protection. That is the sum and substance of the Kṛṣṇa consciousness movement. Everyone is like a plaything in the hands of the illusory energy and is acting as she dictates. One should come to Kṛṣṇa consciousness to release oneself and others from this bondage.

Association with Devotees

These verses lucidly explain how a living entity is victimized by his material conditioning. The beginning of illusion is to misidentify oneself as the body. Therefore the *Bhagavad-gītā* begins with the spiritual instruction that one is not the body but the spirit soul within the body. One can always remain conscious of this fact only if one remains pure by chanting the holy name of Kṛṣṇa, the Hare Kṛṣṇa *mahā-mantra,* and staying in the association of devotees. This is the secret of success. Therefore we stress that one should chant the holy name of the Lord and keep oneself free from the contaminations of this material world, especially the contaminations of lusty desires for illicit sex, meat-eating, intoxication, and gambling. With determination one should vow to follow these principles and thus be saved from the miserable condition of material existence.

The first necessity is to become freed from the bodily conception of life. Ajāmila was immediately freed from the illusory bodily conception of life by hearing the conversation between the Viṣṇudūtas and the Yamadūtas. The proof is that right after this incident he left his wife and children and went straight to Hardwar for further advancement in spiritual life. It is mentioned here that he took shelter in a temple of Viṣṇu and executed the process of devotional service. Our Kṛṣṇa consciousness movement has established temples all over the world for this very purpose. There is no need to travel to Hardwar. Anyone can take shelter of the temple nearest him, engage in the devotional service of the Lord, and thus achieve the highest success in life by becoming absorbed in Kṛṣṇa consciousness.

If one worships the Deity of Kṛṣṇa in the temple, one's mind will naturally be absorbed in thought of the Lord and His form. There is no distinction between the form of the Lord and the Lord Himself. Therefore *bhakti-yoga* is the easiest system of *yoga. Yogīs* try to concentrate their minds upon the form of the Supersoul, Viṣṇu, within the heart, but this same objective is easily achieved when one's mind is absorbed in thinking of the Deity in the temple. In every temple there is a transcendental form of the Lord, and one may easily think of this form. By seeing the Lord during the formal worship ceremony, or *ārati,* by sacrificing one's money, time, and energy for the worship of the Deity, and by constantly thinking of the form of the Deity, one becomes a first-class *yogī.* This is the best process of *yoga,* as confirmed by the Supreme Personality of Godhead in the *Bhagavad-gītā* (6.47):

yoginām api sarveṣāṁ
mad-gatenāntar-ātmanā
śraddhāvān bhajate yo māṁ
sa me yuktatamo mataḥ

"Of all *yogīs,* the one with great faith who always abides in Me, thinks of Me within himself, and renders transcendental loving serve to Me—he is the most intimately united with Me in *yoga* and is the highest of all." So the first-class *yogī* is he who controls his senses and detaches himself from material activities by always thinking of the form of the Lord.

Back to Godhead

The Viṣṇudūtas who had rescued Ajāmila came before him again when his mind was firmly fixed upon the form of the Lord. They had gone away for some time to give Ajāmila a chance to become firmly fixed in meditation upon the Lord. Now that his devotion had matured, they returned to take him back to Godhead. Understanding that the same Viṣṇudūtas had returned, Ajāmila offered them his obeisances by bowing down before them.

Ajāmila was now ready to return home, back to Godhead,

and thus he gave up his material body and regained his original, spiritual body. As the Lord says in the *Bhagavad-gītā* (4.9):

janma karma ca me divyam
evaṁ yo vetti tattvataḥ
tyaktvā dehaṁ punar janma
naiti mām eti so 'rjuna

"One who knows the transcendental nature of My appearance and activities does not, upon leaving the body, take his birth again in this material world, but attains My eternal abode, O Arjuna." The result of perfection in Kṛṣṇa consciousness is that after giving up one's material body, one is immediately transferred to the spiritual world in one's original, spiritual body to become an associate of the Supreme Personality of Godhead. Some devotees go to Vaikuṇṭha to become associates of Lord Viṣṇu, and others go to Goloka Vṛndāvana to become associates of Kṛṣṇa.

Spiritual airplanes from the spiritual planets, like the one that came for Ajāmila, can take one back home, back to Godhead, in a second. The speed of such a spiritual airplane can only be imagined. Spirit is finer than the mind, and everyone has experience of how swiftly the mind travels from one place to another. Therefore one can imagine the swiftness of the spiritual form by comparing it to the speed of the mind. In less than even a moment, a perfect devotee can return home, back to Godhead, immediately after giving up his material body.

Such perfection is not available to anyone but devotees of the Lord. It has been seen that even after achieving so-called perfection, many *karmīs, jñānīs,* and *yogīs* become attached to material activities again. Many so-called *svāmīs* and *yogīs* give up material activities as false (*jagan mithyā*), but after some time they nevertheless resume material activities by opening hospitals and schools or performing other activities for the benefit of the public. Sometimes they participate in politics, although still falsely declaring themselves *sannyāsīs,* members of the renounced order. All these activities are illusory aspects of the material world.

If one actually desires to get out of the material world, he must take to devotional service, which begins with *śravaṇaṁ kīrtanaṁ viṣṇoḥ:* chanting and hearing the glories of the Lord. The Kṛṣṇa consciousness movement has actually proved this. In the Western countries, many young boys and girls who had been addicted to drugs and who had other bad habits, which they could not give up, abandoned all those propensities and very seriously engaged in chanting the glories of the Lord as soon as they joined the Kṛṣṇa consciousness movement. In other words, this process is the perfect method of atonement for actions performed in the modes of passion and ignorance. The *Śrīmad-Bhāgavatam* (1.2.19) confirms this:

> *tadā rajas-tamo-bhāvāḥ*
> *kāma-lobhādayaś ca ye*
> *ceta etair anāviddhaṁ*
> *sthitaṁ sattve prasīdati*

As a result of acting under the modes of passion and ignorance, one becomes increasingly lusty and greedy, but when one takes to the process of chanting and hearing about Kṛṣṇa, one comes to the platform of goodness and becomes happy. As he advances in devotional service, all his doubts are completely eradicated (*bhidyate hṛdaya-granthiś chidyante sarva-saṁśayāḥ*). Thus the knot of his desire for fruitive activities is cut to pieces.

At the time of death one is certainly bewildered because his bodily functions are disordered. At that time, even one who throughout his life has practiced chanting the holy name of the Lord may not be able to chant the Hare Kṛṣṇa *mantra* very distinctly. Nevertheless, such a person receives all the benefits of chanting the holy name. While the body is fit, therefore, why should we not chant the holy name of the Lord loudly and distinctly? If a person does so, it is quite possible that even at the time of death he will be able to properly chant the holy name of the Lord with love and faith. In conclusion, one who chants the holy name of the Lord constantly is guaranteed to return home, back to Godhead, without a doubt.

4

YAMARĀJA'S INSTRUCTIONS ON THE HOLY NAME

CHAPTER 19

Erasing All Doubts

King Parīkṣit said, "O my lord, O Śukadeva Gosvāmī, Yamarāja is the controller of all living entities in terms of their religious and irreligious activities, but his order had been foiled. When his servants, the Yamadūtas, informed him of their defeat by the Viṣṇudūtas, what did he reply?

"O great sage, never before has it been heard anywhere that an order from Yamarāja has been baffled. Therefore I think that people will have doubts about this that no one but you can eradicate. Since that is my firm conviction, kindly explain the reasons for these events."

Śrī Śukadeva Gosvāmī replied: My dear king, when the order-carriers of Yamarāja were baffled and defeated by the order-carriers of Viṣṇu, they approached their master, the controller of Saṁyamanī-purī and master of sinful persons, to tell him of this incident.

The Yamadūtas said, "Our dear lord, how many controllers are there in this material world? How many causes are responsible for manifesting the various results of activities performed under the three modes of material nature?

"If in this universe there are many judges who disagree about punishment and reward, their contradictory actions will neutralize one another, and no one will be punished or rewarded. Otherwise, if their contradictory acts fail to neutralize one another, everyone will have to be both punished and rewarded. Since there are many different *karmīs*, or fruitive workers, there may be different judges to give them justice, but just as one central emperor controls

different departmental rulers, there must be one supreme controller to guide all the judges.

"The supreme judge must be one, not many. It was our understanding that you are that supreme judge and that you have jurisdiction even over the demigods. Our impression was that you are the master of all living entities, the supreme authority who discriminates between the pious and impious activities of all human beings.

"But now we see that the punishment ordained under your authority is no longer effective, since your order has been transgressed by four wonderful and perfect persons. We were bringing the most sinful Ajāmila toward the hellish planets, following your order, when those beautiful persons from Siddhaloka forcibly cut the knots of the ropes with which we were arresting him. As soon as the sinful Ajāmila uttered the name Nārāyaṇa, these four beautiful men immediately arrived and reassured him, saying, 'Do not fear. Do not fear.' We wish to know about them from your lordship. If you think we are able to understand them, kindly describe who they are."

Śrī Śukadeva Gosvāmī said: Thus having been questioned, Lord Yamarāja was very pleased with his order-carriers because of hearing from them the holy name of Nārāyaṇa. He remembered the lotus feet of the Lord and began to reply. (*Śrīmad-Bhāgavatam* 6.3.1–11)

Who's in Charge?

Mahārāja Parīkṣit became astonished and asked Śukadeva Gosvāmī, "How is it possible for anyone to surpass the order of Yamarāja?" Nobody can supersede a warrant issued by the police magistrate. Similarly, Yamarāja is the chief of the universal "police," and he acts on behalf of the Supreme Personality of Godhead, Kṛṣṇa. Yamarāja's business is to arrest all the criminal living entities and subject them to punishment in his region, Yamaloka. Sinful persons are taken there and put into various hellish conditions. The case of Ajāmila, however, is exceptional. The

Yamadūtas were ordered to arrest him and bring him to the court of Yamarāja, but the Viṣṇudūtas released him from their grasp.

The Viṣṇudūtas' interference with the Yamadūtas was apparently unlawful, but just as Lord Viṣṇu can do anything, His messengers can likewise nullify any order in the material world. That is the power of the Supreme Lord. In the material world no one has the authority or power to check the orders of Yamarāja, but the Viṣṇudūtas acted under the higher authority of the Supreme Lord.

When the Yamadūtas returned to Yamaloka, they immediately went to Yamarāja and asked, "How is it that we were checked from carrying out our duty? My dear lord, how many controllers are there? Are you the only contoller, or are there many other controllers?" Less intelligent men think that a particular demigod, such as Indra, Sūrya, or Candra, is supreme. This is like thinking the policeman on the street is all-powerful within the state. There are so many police constables controlling the crowd in the street, but only foolish persons do not understand that above the constables are many higher officers, all the way up to the police commissioner, the governor of the state, and the president. The Yamadūtas simply carried out the orders of Yamarāja, thinking him to be the supreme controller, and this was the first incident in which they were stopped from executing his orders.

Śrīla Viśvanātha Cakravartī Ṭhākura says that the Yamadūtas were so disappointed that it was almost with anger that they asked Yamarāja whether there were many masters other than him. Furthermore, because the Yamadūtas had been defeated and their master could not protect them, they were inclined to say that there was no need to serve such a master. If a servant cannot carry out the orders of his master without being defeated, what is the use of serving such a powerless master?

Because the Yamadūtas had been stopped, they doubted whether Yamarāja actually had the power to punish the sinful. Although they had gone to arrest Ajāmila, following Yamarāja's order, they found themselves unsuccessful because of the order of some higher authority. Therefore they were unsure of whether there were many authorities or only one. If there were many authorities who gave different judgments, which could be contradictory, a person might be wrongly punished or wrongly rewarded, or he might be neither punished nor rewarded. According to our experience in the material world, a person punished in one court may appeal to another. Thus the same man may be either punished or rewarded according to different judgments. However, in the law of nature or the court of the Supreme Personality of Godhead, there cannot be such contradictory judgments. The judges and their judgments must be perfect and free from contradictions.

Actually, the position of Yamarāja was very awkward in the case of Ajāmila because according to everything they had been taught by Yamaraja, the Yamadūtas were right in attempting to arrest Ajāmila, but the Viṣṇudūtas had baffled them. Although Yamarāja, under these circumstances, was accused by both the Viṣṇudūtas and the Yamadūtas, he is perfect in administering justice because he is empowered by the Supreme Personality of Godhead. Therefore he will explain what his real position is and how everyone is controlled by the supreme controller, the Personality of Godhead.

In this world there must be measures for controlling the living entities. *Śāstra,* or scripture, is meant for controlling civilized men. From this word comes the word *śiṣya,* meaning disciple, or one who voluntarily accepts the control or guidance of the spiritual master. Those who are not gentle must be controlled by *astra,* or weapons. The police force needs guns and clubs to control the thieves and rogues of society.

The Yamadūtas inquired from their master whether there are different departments of justice for different types of men. In the material world a person is contaminated by some combination of the three qualities of nature—goodness, passion, and ignorance—and he conducts his activities accordingly. Symptoms of one chiefly under the influence of the mode of ignorance are laziness, excessive sleeping, and uncleanliness. The main symptom of one chiefly under the influence of the mode of passion is a strong desire to exploit material nature and other living entities for one's own sense enjoyment. And the chief symptom of one under the influence of the mode of goodness is knowing things as they are. To such a person, everything is revealed in its proper way.

The Yamadūtas suggested, "There may be many controllers of people in the different modes of nature, but who is the chief controller, and how are his actions carried out? As far as we know, you are the controller of everyone." In governmental management there may be departmental officials to give justice to different persons, but the law must be one, and that central law must control everyone. The Yamadūtas could not imagine that two judges would give two different verdicts in the same case, and therefore they wanted to know who the supreme judge is. The Yamadūtas were certain that Ajāmila was a most sinful man, but although Yamarāja wanted to punish him, the Viṣṇudūtas excused him. This was a puzzling situation that the Yamadūtas wanted Yamarāja to clarify. The Yamadūtas had thought that Yamarāja was the only person in charge of administering justice. They were fully confident that no one could counteract his judgments, but now, to their surprise, his order had been violated by the four wonderful persons from Siddhaloka. Śrīla Viśvanātha Cakravartī Ṭhākura suggests that the Yamadūtas may have said to Yamarāja, "We think that your absolute power of controlling is finished, because four very wonderful personalities checked us from executing our duty, which you gave us."

Viśvanātha Cakravartī also remarks that the Yamadūtas may have wanted to bring the Viṣṇudūtas before Yamarāja. If Yamarāja could then have punished the Viṣṇudūtas, the

Yamadūtas would have been satisfied. Otherwise, they desired to commit suicide. Before pursuing either course, however, they wanted to know about the Viṣṇudūtas from Yamarāja, who is also omniscient.

Submissive Inquiry

The Yamadūtas said, "We wish to learn from you what are the actual facts regarding this incident. If you think that we shall be able to understand, please enlighten us." This is the way of inquiring submissively from superiors. Not challenging. We shall always find that Mahārāja Parīkṣit, Arjuna, and anyone else executing this process of spiritual enlightenment inquires with humble submission and a mood of service. Merely because we put a question to our superior does not mean that he is obliged to answer us. Sometimes he may refuse if we are not able to comprehend the answer. We cannot demand. Inquiry, submission, and service are the way to knowledge. Whenever Mahārāja Parīkṣit questioned Śukadeva Gosvāmī, he said very submissively, "If you think that I shall be able to understand, please answer this question."

Before Yamarāja replied to the Yamadūtas, he first remembered the lotus feet of the Supreme Personality of Godhead, Kṛṣṇa. Just as the subordinate puts the question to his superior with a submissive attitude, similarly, the superior is not proud, boasting, "Yes, I can answer your question!" He remembers the lotus feet of the Lord and prays, "Whatever You help me to speak, I'll answer." As long as the teacher is not proud and the disciple is not disobedient, puffed up, or impudent, they can exchange spiritual questions and answers. One should not inquire in a challenging mood, and the one who answers should remember the lotus feet of the Lord so that the right answer will be given.

Yamarāja was very pleased with his servants because they had chanted the holy name of Nārāyaṇa in his dominion. Yamarāja has to deal with men who are all sinful and who can hardly understand Nārāyaṇa. Consequently, when his order-carriers uttered the name of Nārāyaṇa, he was extremely pleased, for he is also a Vaiṣṇava.

CHAPTER 20

Under One Master

Yamarāja said, "My dear servants, you have accepted me as the Supreme, but factually I am not. Above me, and above all the other demigods, including Indra and Candra, is the one supreme master and controller. The partial manifestations of His personality are Brahmā, Viṣṇu, and Śiva, who are in charge of the creation, maintenance, and annihilation of this universe. He is like the two threads that form the length and breadth of a woven cloth.

"Just as the driver of a bullock cart ties ropes through the nostrils of his bulls to control them, the Supreme Personality of Godhead binds all men with the ropes of His words in the *Vedas*, which set forth the names and activities of the distinct orders of human society (*brāhmaṇa, kṣatriya, vaiśya,* and *śūdra*). In fear, the members of these orders all worship the Supreme Lord by offering Him presentations according to their respective activities.

"I, Yamarāja; Indra, the King of heaven; Nirṛti; Varuṇa, the god of the waters; Candra, the moon-god; Agni, the fire-god; Lord Śiva; Pavana, the god of the air; Lord Brahmā; Sūrya, the sun-god; Viśvāsu; the eight Vasus; the Sādhyas; the Maruts; the Rudras; the Siddhas; and Marīci and the other great *ṛṣis* engaged in maintaining the departmental affairs of the universe, as well as the best of the demigods headed by Bṛhaspati and the great sages headed by Bhṛgu, are all certainly freed from the influence of the two base material modes of nature, namely passion and ignorance. Nevertheless, although we are in the mode of

goodness, we cannot understand the activities of the Supreme Personality of Godhead. What, then, is to be said of others, who under illusion merely speculate to know God?

"As the different limbs of the body cannot see the eyes, so the living entities cannot see the Supreme Lord, who is situated as the Supersoul in everyone's heart. Not by the senses, by the mind, by the life air, by thoughts within the heart, or by the vibration of words can the living entities ascertain the real situation of the Supreme Lord." (*Śrīmad-Bhāgavatam* 6.3.12–16)

One Supreme Controller

The Yamadūtas suspected that there was a ruler even above Yamarāja. To eradicate their doubts, Yamarāja immediately replied, "Yes, there is one supreme controller above everything." Yamarāja is in charge of some of the moving living entities, namely the human beings, but the animals, who also move, are not under his control. Only human beings have consciousness of right and wrong, and among them only those who perform sinful activities come under the control of Yamarāja. Therefore although Yamarāja is a controller, he is only a departmental controller of a few living entities. There are other demigods who control many other departments, but above them all is one supreme controller, Kṛṣṇa. *Īśvaraḥ paramaḥ kṛṣṇaḥ:* the supreme controller is Kṛṣṇa. Others, who control their own departments in the affairs of the universe, are insignificant in comparison to Kṛṣṇa, the supreme controller. As Kṛṣṇa says in the *Bhagavad-gītā* (7.7), *mattaḥ parataraṁ nānyat kiñcid asti dhanañjaya:* "My dear Dhanañjaya [Arjuna], no one is superior to Me." Therefore Yamarāja immediately cleared away the doubts of his assistants, the Yamadūtas, by confirming that there is a supreme controller above all others.

In this material world, everyone is controlled by the laws of nature, regardless of who he is. Whether one is a human being, a demigod, an animal, a tree, or a plant, one is controlled by the laws of nature, and behind this natural control is the Supreme Personality of Godhead. Kṛṣṇa confirms this in the *Bhagavad-gītā* (9.10): *mayādhyakṣeṇa prakṛtiḥ sūyate sa-carācaram.* "The material nature is working under My direction and producing all moving and nonmoving beings." Thus the natural machine works under Kṛṣṇa's control.

Under the Control of Varṇa and Āśrama

Apart from other living entities, a living being in the human form of body is meant to be controlled by the Vedic injunctions in terms of the divisions of *varṇa* and *āśrama,* the social and spiritual classes. Otherwise he cannot escape punishment by Yamarāja. The point is that every human being is expected to elevate himself to the position of a *brāhmaṇa,* the most intelligent man, and then one must transcend that position to become a Vaiṣṇava. This is the perfection of life. The *brāhmaṇas, kṣatriyas, vaiśyas,* and *śūdras* can elevate themselves by worshiping the Lord according to their activities (*sve sve kurmaṇy abhiratah saṁsiddhiṁ labhate naraḥ*). The divisions of *varṇa* and *āśrama* are necessary to insure the proper execution of duties and peaceful existence for everyone, but everyone is directed to worship the Supreme Lord, who is all-pervading (*yena sarvam idaṁ tatam*). If one thus follows the Vedic injunctions by worshiping the Supreme Lord according to one's ability, his life will be perfect. The *Śrīmad-Bhāgavatam* (1.2.13) confirms this:

ataḥ pumbhir dvija-śreṣṭha
varṇāśrama-vibhāgaśaḥ
svanuṣṭhitasya dharmasya
saṁsiddhir hari-toṣaṇam

"O best among the twice-born, it is therefore concluded that the highest perfection one can achieve by discharging one's prescribed duties (*dharma*) according to caste divisions and orders of life is to please the Personality of Godhead." The *varṇāśrama* institution offers the perfect process for making one eligible to return home, back to Godhead, because the aim of every *varṇa* and *āśrama* is to please the Lord. One can please the Lord under the direction of a bona fide spiritual master, and then one's life is perfect. The Supreme Lord is worshipable, and everyone worships Him directly or indirectly. Those who worship Him directly get the results of liberation quickly, whereas the liberation of those who serve Him indirectly is delayed.

The words *nāmabhir vāci* in verse 13 (*nāmabhiḥ*—by different names; *vāci*—to the Vedic language) are very important. In the *varṇāśrama* institution, there are different names—*brāhmaṇa, kṣatriya, vaiśya, śūdra, brahmacārī, gṛhastha, vānaprastha,* and *sannyāsī.* The *vāk,* or Vedic injunctions, give directions for all these divisions. Everyone is expected to offer obeisances to the Supreme Lord and perform duties as indicated in the *Vedas.*

Controlled by Three Modes of Nature

Men and other living entities within this cosmic manifestation are controlled by the three modes of nature. For the living entities controlled by the base qualities of nature—passion and ignorance—there is no possibility of understanding God. Even those in the mode of goodness, like the many demigods and great *ṛṣis* described in these verses, cannot understand the activities of the Supreme Personality of Godhead. As stated in the *Bhagavad-gītā,* only one who is situated in devotional service to the Lord, and who is thus transcendental to all material qualities, can understand Him (*bhaktyā mām abhijānāti*).

Ordinary philosophers can never know the Lord. The great devotee Bhīṣmadeva confirms this in the following statement to Mahārāja Yudhiṣṭhira (*Śrīmad-Bhāgavatam* 1.9.16):

na hy asya karhicid rājan
pumān veda vidhitsitam

yad-vijijñāsayā yuktā
muhyanti kavayo 'pi hi

"O king, no one can know the plan of the Lord, Śrī Kṛṣṇa. Even though great philosophers inquire exhaustively, they are bewildered." No one, therefore, can understand God by speculative knowledge. Indeed, by speculation one will be bewildered.

Directed by the Supersoul

Although the different parts of the body do not have the power to see the eyes, the eyes direct the movements of the body's different parts. The legs move forward because the eyes see what is in front of them, and the hand touches because the eyes see touchable entities. Similarly, every living being acts according to the direction of the Supersoul, who is situated within the heart. The Lord Himself confirms this in the *Bhagavad-gītā* (15.15): *sarvasya cāhaṁ hṛdi sanniviṣṭho mattaḥ smṛtir jñānam apohanaṁ ca.* "I am sitting in everyone's heart and giving directions for remembrance, knowledge, and forgetfulness." Elsewhere in the *Bhagavad-gītā* (18.61) it is stated, *īśvaraḥ sarva-bhūtānāṁ hṛd-deśe 'rjuna tiṣṭhati:* "The Supreme Lord, as the Supersoul, is situated in the heart." The living entity cannot do anything without the sanction of the Supersoul. The Supersoul is acting at every moment, but the living entity cannot understand the form and activities of the Supersoul by manipulating his senses. The example of the eyes and the bodily limbs is very appropriate. If the limbs could see, they could walk forward without the help of the eyes; but that is impossible. Although one cannot see the Supersoul in one's heart through sensual activities, His direction is necessary.

CHAPTER 21

Confidential Knowledge

Yamarāja continued: "The Supreme Personality of Godhead is self-sufficient and fully independent. He is the master of everyone and everything, including the illusory energy. He has His form, qualities, and features, and similarly His order-carriers, the Viṣṇudūtas, or Vaiṣṇavas, who are very beautiful, possess bodily features and transcendental qualities almost like His. They always wander within this world with full independence.

"The Viṣṇudūtas are worshiped even by the demigods and are very rarely seen. They protect the devotees of the Lord from the hands of enemies, from envious persons, and even from my jurisdiction, as well as from natural disturbances.

"The real religious principle is enacted by the Supreme Personality of Godhead. Although fully situated in the mode of goodness, even the great *ṛṣis* who occupy the topmost planets cannot ascertain this principle, nor can the demigods or the leaders of Siddhaloka, to say nothing of the demons, ordinary human beings, Vidyādharas, or Cāraṇas.

"Lord Brahmā, Bhagavān Nārada, Lord Śiva, the four Kumāras, Lord Kapila [the son of Devahūti], Svāyambhuva Manu, Prahlāda Mahārāja, Janaka Mahārāja, Grandfather Bhīṣma, Bali Mahārāja, Śukadeva Gosvāmī, and I myself know the real religious principle. My dear servants, this transcendental religious principle, which is known as *bhāgavata-dharma*, or surrender unto the Supreme Lord and love for Him, is uncontaminated by the material modes of nature. It is very confidential and difficult for ordinary human beings to understand, but if by chance one fortunately understands it, he is immediately liberated, and thus he returns home, back to Godhead.

"Devotional service, beginning with the chanting of the holy name of the Lord, is the ultimate religious principle for the living entity in human society.

"My dear servants, who are as good as my sons, just see how glorious is the chanting of the holy name of the Lord! The greatly sinful Ajāmila chanted only to call his son, not knowing that he was chanting the Lord's holy name. Nevertheless, by chanting the holy name of the Lord he remembered Nārāyaṇa, and thus he was immediately saved from the ropes of death.

"Therefore it should be understood that one is easily relieved from all sinful reactions by chanting the holy name of the Lord and chanting His qualities and activities. This is the only process recommended for relief from sinful reactions. Even if a person chants the holy name of the Lord with improper pronunciation, he will achieve relief from material bondage if he chants without offenses. Ajāmila, for example, was extremely sinful, but while dying he merely chanted the holy name, and although calling his son, he achieved complete liberation because he remembered the name of Nārāyaṇa.

"Because they are bewildered by the Supreme Lord's illusory energy, Yājñavalkya, Jaimini, and other compilers of the religious scriptures cannot know the confidential religious system of the twelve *mahājanas*. They cannot understand the transcendental value of performing devotional service or chanting the Hare Kṛṣṇa *mantra*. Because their minds are attracted to the ritualistic ceremonies mentioned in the *Vedas*—especially the *Yajur Veda, Sāma Veda,* and *Ṛg Veda*—their intelligence has become dull. Thus they are busy collecting the ingredients for ritualistic ceremonies that yield only temporary benefits, such as elevation to

Svargaloka for material happiness. They are not attracted to the *saṅkīrtana* movement; instead, they are interested in religiosity, economic development, sense gratification, and liberation.

"Considering all these points, therefore, intelligent men decide to solve all problems by adopting the devotional service of chanting the holy name of the Lord, who is situated in everyone's heart and who is a mine of all auspicious qualities. Such persons are not within my jurisdiction for punishment. Generally they never commit sinful activities, but even if by mistake or because of bewilderment or illusion they sometimes commit sinful acts, they are protected from sinful reactions because they always chant the Hare Kṛṣṇa *mantra.*

"My dear servants, please do not approach such devotees, for they have fully surrendered to the lotus feet of the Supreme Personality of Godhead. They are equal to everyone, and their narrations are sung by the demigods and the inhabitants of Siddhaloka. Please do not even go near them. They are always protected by the club of the Supreme Lord, and therefore Lord Brahmā and I and even the time factor are not competent to chastise them.

"*Paramahaṁsas* are exalted persons who have no taste for material enjoyment and who drink the honey of the Lord's lotus feet. My dear servants, bring to me for punishment only persons who are averse to the taste of that honey, who do not associate with *paramahaṁsas,* and who are attached to family life and worldly enjoyment, which form the path to hell.

"My dear servants, please bring to me only those sinful persons who do not use their tongues to chant the holy name and qualities of Kṛṣṇa, whose hearts do not remember the lotus feet of Kṛṣṇa even once, and whose heads do not bow down even once before Lord Kṛṣṇa. Send me those who do not perform their duties toward Viṣṇu, which are the only duties in human life. Please bring me all such fools and rascals." (*Śrīmad-Bhāgavatam* 6.3.17–29)

The Protectors

Yamarāja was describing the Supreme Personality of Godhead, the supreme controller, but the order-carriers of Yamarāja were very eager to know about the Viṣṇudūtas, who had defeated them in their encounter with Ajāmila. Yamarāja therefore stated that the Viṣṇudūtas resemble the Supreme Personality of Godhead in their bodily features, transcendental qualities, and nature. In other words, the Viṣṇudūtas, or Vaiṣṇavas, are almost as qualified as the Supreme Lord. Yamarāja informed the Yamadūtas that the Viṣṇudūtas are no less powerful than Lord Viṣṇu. Since Viṣṇu is above Yamarāja, the Viṣṇudūtas are above the Yamadūtas. Persons protected by the Viṣṇudūtas, therefore, cannot be touched by the Yamadūtas.

Yamarāja has described the qualities of the Viṣṇudūtas to convince his own servants not to be envious of them. Yamarāja warned the Yamadūtas that the Viṣṇudūtas are worshiped with respectful obeisances by the demigods and are always very alert to protect the devotees of the Lord from the hands of enemies, from natural disturbances, and from all dangerous conditions in this material world. Sometimes the members of the Kṛṣṇa consciousness society are afraid of the impending danger of world war and ask what would happen to them if a war should occur. In all kinds of danger they should be confident of their protection by the Viṣṇudūtas or the Supreme Personality of Godhead, as Kṛṣṇa Himself confirms in the *Bhagavad-gītā* (9.31): *kaunteya pratijānīhi na me bhaktaḥ praṇaśyati.* "O son of Kuntī, declare it boldly that My devotee never perishes."

Material danger is not meant for devotees. This is also confirmed in the *Śrīmad-Bhāgavatam* (10.14.58): *padaṁ padaṁ yad vipadāṁ na teṣām.* In this material world there are dangers at every step, but they are not meant for devotees who have fully surrendered unto the lotus feet of the Lord. The pure devotees of Lord Viṣṇu may rest assured that the Lord will protect them, and as long as they are in this material world they should fully engage in devotional service by preaching the message of Śrī Caitanya Mahāprabhu and Lord Kṛṣṇa, namely chanting Hare Kṛṣṇa and the other aspects of Kṛṣṇa consciousness.

Direct Connection with Kṛṣṇa

When challenged by the Viṣṇudūtas to describe the principles of religion, the Yamadūtas had said, *veda-praṇihito dharmaḥ:* "The Vedic literature defines religious principles." They did not know, however, that the Vedic literature contains ritualistic ceremonies that are not transcendental but are meant to keep peace and order among materialistic persons in the material world. Real religious principles are *nistraiguṇya*, above the three modes of material nature, or transcendental. The Yamadūtas did not know these transcendental religious principles, and therefore when prevented from arresting Ajāmila, they were surprised.

Materialistic persons who attach all their faith to the Vedic rituals are described in the *Bhagavad-gītā* (2.42), wherein Kṛṣṇa says, *veda-vāda-ratāḥ pārtha nānyad astīti vādinaḥ:* "The supposed followers of the *Vedas* say that there is nothing beyond the Vedic ceremonies." Indeed, there is a group of men in India who are very fond of the Vedic rituals, not understanding the meaning of these rituals, which are intended to elevate one gradually to the transcendental platform of knowing Kṛṣṇa (*vedaiś ca sarvair aham eva vedyaḥ*). Those who do not know this principle but who simply attach their faith to the Vedic rituals are called *veda-vāda-ratāḥ*.

Herein it is stated that the real religious principle is that which is given by the Supreme Personality of Godhead. Lord Kṛṣṇa states that principle in the *Bhagavad-gītā* (18.66): *sarva-dharmān parityajya mām ekaṁ śaraṇaṁ vraja.* "Give up all other duties and surrender unto Me." That is the real religious principle everyone should follow. Even though one follows the Vedic scriptures, one may not know this transcendental principle, for it is not known to everyone. To say nothing of human beings, even the demigods in the upper planetary systems are unaware of it. This transcendental religious principle must be understood from the Supreme Personality of Godhead directly or from His special representative, as stated in these verses.

In the *Bhagavad-gītā* Lord Kṛṣṇa refers to *bhāgavata-dharma* as the most confidential religious principle (*sarva-guhyatamam, guhyād guhyataram*). Kṛṣṇa says to Arjuna, "Because you are My very dear friend, I am explaining to you the most confidential religion." *Sarva-dharmān parityajya mām ekaṁ śaraṇaṁ vraja:* "Give up all other duties and surrender unto Me." One may ask, If this principle is very rarely understood, what is the use of it? In answer, Yamarāja states herein that this religious principle is understandable if one follows the *paramparā* system of Lord Brahmā, Lord Śiva, the four Kumāras, and the other standard authorities. There are four lines of disciplic succession: one from Lord Brahmā, one from Lord Śiva, one from Lakṣmī, the goddess of fortune, and one from the Kumāras. The disciplic succession from Lord Brahmā is called the Brahma-sampradāya, the succession from Lord Śiva (Śambhu) is called the Rudra-sampradāya, the one from the goddess of fortune, Lakṣmīji, is called the Śrī-sampradāya, and the one from the Kumāras is called the Kumāra-sampradāya. One must take shelter of one of these four *sampradāyas* in order to understand the most confidential religious system. In the *Padma Purāṇa* it is said, *sampradāya-vihīnā ye mantras te niṣphalā matāḥ:* if one does not follow the four recognized disciplic successions, his *mantra,* or initiation, is useless.

At present there are many *apasampradāyas,* or un–bona fide *sampradāyas,* which have no link to authorities like Lord Brahmā, Lord Śiva, the Kumāras, or Lakṣmī. People are misguided by such *sampradāyas.* The *śāstras* say that being initiated into such a *sampradāya* is a waste of time, for it will never enable one to understand real religious principles and surrender to Kṛṣṇa.

Real religious principles are *bhāgavata-dharma,* the principles described in the *Śrīmad-Bhāgavatam* itself or in the *Bhagavad-gītā,* the preliminary study of the *Bhāgavatam.* What are these principles? The *Bhāgavatam* (1.1.2) says, *dharmaḥ projjhita-kaitavo 'tra:* "In the *Śrīmad-Bhāgavatam* there are no cheating religious systems." In other words, everything in the *Bhāgavatam* is directly connected with the Supreme Personality of Godhead. The *Bhāgavatam* (1.2.6) further says, *sa vai puṁsāṁ paro dharmo yato bhaktir adhokṣaje:* "The supreme religion is that which teaches its followers how to love the Supreme Personality of Godhead, who is beyond the reach of experimental knowledge." Such a religious system begins with *tan-nāma-grahaṇa,* chanting the holy name of the Lord. After chanting the holy name and dancing in ecstasy, one gradually sees the transcendental form of the Lord, the qualities of the Lord, and the pastimes of the Lord. In this way one fully understands the situation of the Personality of Godhead.

One can come to this understanding of the Lord, however, only by executing devotional service. As Kṛṣṇa states in the *Bhagavad-gītā* (18.55), *bhaktyā mām abhijānāti yāvān yaś cāsmi tattvataḥ:* "One can understand Me as I am only by devotional service." If a person is fortunate enough to understand the Supreme Lord in this way, the result is that after giving up his material body he no longer has to take birth in this material world (*tyaktvā dehaṁ punar janma naiti*). Instead, he returns home, back to Godhead. That is the ultimate perfection. Therefore Kṛṣṇa says in the *Bhagavad-gītā* (8.15):

mām upetya punar janma
duḥkhālayam aśāśvatam
nāpnuvanti mahātmānaḥ
saṁsiddhiṁ paramāṁ gatāḥ

"After attaining Me, the great souls, who are *yogīs* in devotion, never return to this temporary world, which is full of miseries, because they have attained the highest perfection."

Evidence in Support of Chanting the Holy Name

There is no need to conduct research into the significance of the chanting of the Hare Kṛṣṇa *mantra.* The history of Ajāmila is sufficient proof of the power of the Lord's holy name and the exalted position of a person who chants the holy name incessantly. Therefore Śrī Caitanya Mahāprabhu advised,

harer nāma harer nāma
harer nāmaiva kevalam
kalau nāsty eva nāsty eva
nāsty eva gatir anyathā

"In this age of quarrel and hypocrisy, the only means of deliverance is chanting the holy name of the Lord. There is no other way. There is no other way. There is no other way." (*Bṛhan-nāradīya Purāṇa* 3.8.126) In this age, almost no one can perform all the difficult ritualistic ceremonies for becoming liberated. Therefore all the *śāstras* and all the *ācāryas* have recommended that in this age one simply chant the holy name. That will bring one all perfection.

In the assembly of Raghunātha dāsa Gosvāmī's father, Haridāsa Ṭhākura confirmed that simply by chanting the Lord's holy name a person is liberated, even if he does not chant completely inoffensively. *Smārta-brāhmaṇas* and Māyāvādīs do not believe that one can achieve liberation in this way, but the truth of Haridāsa Ṭhākura's statement is supported by many quotations from the Vedic literature.

In the passage of *Śrīmad-Bhāgavatam* under discussion, for example, Yamarāja says, "It should be understood that one is easily relieved from all sinful reactions by chanting the holy name of the Lord and chanting His qualities and activities. This is the only process recommended for relief from sinful reactions." In his commentary on this verse, Śrīdhara Svāmī gives the following quotation: *sāyaṁ prātar gṛṇan bhaktyā duḥkha-grāmād vimucyate.* "If one continually chants the holy name of the Lord with great devotion morning and evening, one will become free from all material miseries." Another quotation confirms that a person can achieve liberation if he hears the holy name of the Lord continually, every day, with great respect: *anudinam idam ādareṇa śṛṇvan.* Another quotation says,

śravaṇaṁ kīrtanaṁ dhyānaṁ
harer adbhuta-karmaṇaḥ
janma-karma-guṇānāṁ ca
tad-arthe 'khila-ceṣṭitam

"One should always chant and hear about the wonderful activities of the Lord, one should meditate upon these activities, and one should endeavor to please the Lord." (*Śrīmad-Bhāgavatam* 11.3.27) Śrīdhara Svāmī also gives the following quote from the *Purāṇas: pāpa-kṣayaś ca bhavati smaratāṁ tam ahar-niśam.* "One can become free from all sinful reactions simply by remembering the lotus feet of the Lord day and night." Finally, he quotes from the chapter of *Śrīmad-Bhāgavatam* under discussion (6.3.31):

tasmāt saṅkīrtanaṁ viṣṇor
jagan-maṅgalam aṁhasām
mahatām api kauravya
viddhy aikāntika-niṣkṛtam

"The chanting of the holy name of the Lord is able to uproot even the reactions of the greatest sins. Therefore the chanting of the *saṅkīrtana* movement is the most auspicious activity in the entire universe."

All these quotations prove that one who constantly engages in chanting and hearing the holy name of the Lord, along with descriptions of His fame, form, and activities, is liberated. As stated wonderfully in verse 24, *etāvatālam agha-nirharaṇāya puṁsām:* simply by uttering the name of the Lord, one is freed from all sinful reactions.

The word *alam* in this verse indicates that simply uttering the holy name of the Lord is sufficient. There is no need of any other process. Even if a person chants imperfectly, he becomes free from all sinful reactions.

The liberation of Ajāmila proves this power of chanting the holy name. When Ajāmila chanted the holy name of Nārāyaṇa, he did not precisely remember the Supreme Lord; instead, he remembered his own son. At the time of death, Ajāmila certainly was not very clean; indeed, he was famous as a great sinner. Furthermore, one's physiological condition is completely disturbed at the time of death, and in such an awkward condition it would certainly have been very difficult for Ajāmila to have chanted clearly. Nevertheless, Ajāmila achieved liberation simply by chanting the holy name of the Lord. Therefore, what is to be said of those who are not sinful like Ajāmila? It is to be concluded that with a strong vow one should chant the holy name of the Lord—Hare Kṛṣṇa, Hare Kṛṣṇa, Kṛṣṇa Kṛṣṇa, Hare Hare/ Hare Rāma, Hare Rāma, Rāma Rāma, Hare Hare—for thus by the grace of Kṛṣṇa one will certainly be delivered from the clutches of *māyā.*

The chanting of the Hare Kṛṣṇa *mantra* is recommended even for persons who commit offenses, because if they continue chanting they will gradually chant offenselessly. Then, by chanting Hare Kṛṣṇa without offenses, one increases his love for Kṛṣṇa. As stated by Lord Caitanya, *premā pum-artho mahān:* one's main concern should be to increase one's attachment to the Supreme Personality of Godhead and to increase one's love for Him.

Since one may easily achieve the highest success by chanting the holy name of the Lord, one may ask why there are so many Vedic ritualistic ceremonies and why people are attracted to them. Yamarāja answers this question in the passage of *Śrīmad-Bhāgavatam* under discussion. Unfortunately, unintelligent people are bewildered by the grandeur of Vedic *yajñas,* and thus they want to see gorgeous sacrifices performed. They want Vedic *mantras* chanted and huge amounts of money spent for such ceremonies. Sometimes we have to observe the Vedic ritualistic ceremonies to please such unintelligent men. In 1975, when we established a large Kṛṣṇa-Balarāma temple in Vṛndāvana, we were obliged to have Vedic ceremonies performed by *brāhmaṇas* because the inhabitants of Vṛndāvana, especially the *smārta-brāhmaṇas,* would not accept Europeans and Americans as bona fide *brāhmaṇas.* Thus we had to engage *brāhmaṇas* to perform costly *yajñas.* As these *yajñas* were being performed, the members of our Society performed *saṅkīrtana* loudly with *mṛdaṅgas,* and I considered the *saṅkīrtana* more important than the Vedic ritualistic ceremonies. The ceremonies and the *saṅkīrtana* were going on simultaneously. The ceremonies were meant for persons interested in Vedic rituals for elevation to heavenly planets (*jaḍī-kṛta-matir madhu-puṣpitāyām*), whereas the *saṅkīrtana* was meant for pure devotees interested in pleasing the Supreme Personality of Godhead. We would simply have performed *saṅkīrtana,* but then the inhabitants of Vṛndāvana would not have taken the installation ceremony seriously. As explained here, the Vedic performances are meant for those whose intelligence has been dulled by the flowery words of the *Vedas,* which describe sacrifices intended to elevate one to the higher planets.

Especially in this age, *saṅkīrtana* alone is sufficient. If the members of our temples in the different parts of the world simply continue *saṅkīrtana* before the Deity, especially before Śrī Caitanya Mahāprabhu, they will remain perfect. There is no need of any other performances. Nevertheless, to keep oneself clean in habits and mind, Deity worship and other regulative principles are required. Śrīla Jiva Gosvāmī says that although *saṅkīrtana* is sufficient for the perfection of life, worship of the Deity in the temple must continue so that the devotees may stay clean and pure. Śrīla Bhaktisiddhānta Sarasvatī Ṭhākura therefore recommended that one follow both processes simultaneously. We strictly follow his principle of performing Deity worship and *saṅkīrtana* along parallel lines. This we should continue.

The Jurisdiction of Yamarāja

In this regard, Śrīla Viśvanātha Cakravartī Ṭhākura quotes the following verse from the prayers of Lord Brahmā (*Śrīmad-Bhāgavatam* 10.14.29):

athāpi te deva padāmbuja-dvaya-
prasāda-leśānugṛhīta eva hi
jānāti tattvaṁ bhagavan-mahimno
na cānya eko 'pi ciraṁ vicinvan

The purport is that even though one is a very learned scholar of the Vedic *śāstras,* he may be completely unaware of the existence of the Supreme Personality of Godhead and His name, fame, qualities, and so forth, whereas one who is not a great scholar can understand the position of the Supreme Personality of Godhead if he somehow or other becomes a pure devotee of the Lord by engaging in devotional service. Therefore in verse 26 Yamarāja says, *evaṁ vimṛśya sudhiyo bhagavati:* those who engage in the loving service of the Lord become *sudhiyaḥ,* intelligent, but this is not so of a Vedic scholar who does not understand Kṛṣṇa's name, fame, and qualities. A pure devotee is one whose intelligence is clear; he is truly thoughtful, because he engages in the service of the Lord—not as a matter of show but with love, with his mind, words, and body. Nondevotees may make a show of religion, but it is not very effective, because although they ostentatiously attend a temple or church, they are thinking of something else. Such persons are neglecting their religious duty and are punishable by Yamarāja. But a devotee who commits sinful acts unwillingly or accidentally, because of his former habits, is excused. That is the value of the *saṅkīrtana* movement.

In effect, Yamarāja warned his servants, "My dear servants, henceforward you must stop disturbing the devotees. The devotees who have surrendered unto the lotus feet of the Lord and who constantly chant His holy name are praised by the demigods and the residents of

Siddhaloka. Those devotees are so respectable and exalted that Lord Viṣṇu personally protects them with the club in His hand. If you approach such devotees, He will kill you with that club. What to speak of you, if even Lord Brahmā or I were to punish them, Lord Viṣṇu would punish us. Therefore do not disturb the devotees any further."

After warning the Yamadūtas in this way, Yamarāja then indicates who is to be brought before him. He specifically advises the Yamadūtas to bring to him materialistic persons attached to household life merely for sex. As stated in the *Śrīmad-Bhāgavatam* (7.9.45), *yan maithunādi-gṛhamedhi-sukhaṁ hi tuccham:* people are attached to household life only for sex pleasure, which is very insignificant. They are always harassed in many ways by their material engagements for making money to maintain their families, and their only happiness is that after working very hard all day, at night they sleep and indulge in sex. Yamarāja specifically advises his servants to bring these persons to him for punishment and not to bring the devotees, who always lick the honey from the lotus feet of the Lord, who are equal to everyone, and who try to preach Kṛṣṇa consciousness out of sympathy for all living entities. Devotees are not liable to be punished by Yamarāja, but persons who have no information of Kṛṣṇa consciousness cannot be protected by their material life of so-called family enjoyment. The *Śrīmad-Bhāgavatam* (2.1.4) says,

dehāpatya-kalatrādiṣv
ātma-sainyeṣv asatsv api
teṣāṁ pramatto nidhanaṁ
paśyann api na paśyati

Materialistic persons complacently believe that their nations, communities, or families can protect them, unaware that all such fallible soldiers will be destroyed in due course of time.

In conclusion, one should try to associate with persons

who engage in devotional service twenty-four hours a day. Then one can come to know the purpose of human life, which is to please Lord Viṣṇu. *Varṇāśrama-dharma* is also meant for that purpose. As stated in the *Viṣṇu Purāṇa* (3.8.9):

varṇāśramācāravatā
puruṣeṇa paraḥ pumān
viṣṇur ārādhyate panthā
nānyat tat-toṣa-kāraṇam

Human society is meant to follow strictly the *varṇāśrama-dharma,* which divides society into four social divisions (*brāhmaṇa, kṣatriya, vaiśya,* and *śūdra*) and four spiritual divisions (*brahmacarya, gṛhastha, vānaprastha,* and *sannyāsa*). *Varṇāśrama-dharma* easily brings one nearer to Lord Viṣṇu, who is the only true objective in human society. *Na te viduḥ svārtha-gatiṁ hi viṣṇum:* unfortunately, however, people do not know that their self-interest is to return home, back to Godhead, or to approach Lord Viṣṇu. *Durāśayā ye bahir-artha māninaḥ:* instead, they are simply bewildered by Kṛṣṇa's external, illusory energy. Every human being is expected to perform duties meant for approaching Lord Viṣṇu. Therefore Yamarāja advises the Yamadūtas to bring him only those persons who have forgotten their duties toward Viṣṇu. One who does not chant the holy name of Viṣṇu or Kṛṣṇa, who does not bow down to the Deity of the Lord, and who does not remember His lotus feet is punishable by Yamarāja. In summary, all *avaiṣṇavas,* persons unconcerned with Lord Viṣṇu, are punishable by Yamarāja.

CHAPTER 22

The Glories Of the Holy Name

[Then Yamarāja, considering himself and his servants offenders, spoke as follows, begging pardon from the Lord:] "O my Lord, my servants have surely committed a great offense by arresting a Vaiṣṇava such as Ajāmila. O Nārāyaṇa, O supreme and oldest person, please forgive us. Because of our ignorance, we failed to recognize Ajāmila as a servant of Your Lordship, and thus we have certainly committed a great offense. Therefore with folded hands we beg Your pardon. My Lord, since You are supremely merciful and are always full of good qualities, please pardon us. We offer our respectful obeisances unto You."

Śukadeva Gosvāmī continued: My dear king, the chanting of the holy name of the Lord is able to uproot even the reactions of the greatest sins. Therefore the chanting of the *saṅkīrtana* movement is the most auspicious activity in the entire universe. Please try to understand this so that others will take it seriously.

One who constantly hears and chants the holy name of the Lord and hears and chants about His activities can very easily attain the platform of pure devotional service, which can cleanse the dirt from one's heart. One cannot achieve such purification merely by observing vows and performing Vedic ritualistic ceremonies.

Devotees who always lick the honey from the lotus feet of Lord Kṛṣṇa do not care at all for material activities,

which are performed under the three modes of nature and which bring only misery. Indeed, devotees never give up the lotus feet of Kṛṣṇa to return to material activities. Others, however, who are addicted to Vedic rituals because they have neglected the service of the Lord's lotus feet and are enchanted by lusty desires, sometimes perform acts of atonement. Nevertheless, being incompletely purified, they return to sinful activities again and again.

After hearing from the mouth of their master about the extraordinary glories of the Lord and His name, fame, and attributes, the Yamadūtas were struck with wonder. Since then, as soon as they see a devotee, they fear him and dare not look at him again.

When the great sage Agastya was residing in the Malaya Hills and worshiping the Supreme Personality of Godhead, I approached him, and he explained to me this confidential history. (*Śrīmad-Bhāgavatam* 6.3.30–35)

Yamarāja Prays for Pardon

Lord Yamarāja took upon himself the responsibility for the offense committed by his servants. If the servant of an establishment makes a mistake, the establishment takes responsibility for it. Although Yamarāja is above offenses, his servants, practically with his permission, went to arrest Ajāmila, which was a great offense. The *nyāya-śāstra* confirms, *bhṛtyāparādhe svāmīno daṇḍaḥ:* "If a servant makes an offense, the master is punishable." Taking this seriously, Yamarāja, along with his servants, prayed with folded hands to be excused by the Supreme Lord, Nārāyaṇa.

Achieving Perfection

We should note that although Ajāmila chanted the name of Nārāyaṇa imperfectly, he was delivered from all sinful reactions. The chanting of the holy name is so auspicious that it can free everyone from the reactions of sinful activities. However, as we have mentioned several times before, no one should conclude that he may continue to sin with the intention of chanting Hare Kṛṣṇa to neutralize the reactions. Rather, one should be very careful to remain free from all sins and never think of counteracting sinful activities by chanting the Hare Kṛṣṇa *mantra*, for this is another offense. If by chance a devotee accidentally performs some sinful activity, the Lord will excuse him, but one should not intentionally perform sinful acts.

One may very easily practice chanting and hearing the holy name of the Lord and thus become ecstatic in spiritual life. The *Padma Purāṇa* states,

nāmāparādha-yuktānāṁ
nāmāny eva haranty agham
aviśrānti-prayuktāni
tāny evārtha-karāṇi ca

Even if one chants the Hare Kṛṣṇa *mantra* offensively, one can nullify these offenses by continuously chanting without deviation. One who becomes accustomed to this practice will always remain in a pure transcendental position, untouchable by sinful reactions.

A devotee's duty is to chant the Hare Kṛṣṇa *mantra.* One may sometimes chant with offenses and sometimes without offenses, but if one seriously adopts this process, he will achieve perfection, which cannot be achieved through Vedic ritualistic ceremonies of atonement. Persons who are attached to the Vedic ritualistic ceremonies but do not believe in devotional service, who advise atonement but do not appreciate the chanting of the Lord's holy name, fail to achieve the highest perfection. Devotees, therefore, being completely detached from material enjoyment, never give up Kṛṣṇa consciousness for Vedic ritualistic ceremonies. Those who are attached to Vedic ritualistic ceremonies because of lusty desires are subjected to the tribulations of material existence again and again.

Since this incident, the Yamadūtas have given up the dangerous behavior of approaching devotees. For the Yamadūtas, a devotee is dangerous.

APPENDIXES

The Author

His Divine Grace A. C. Bhaktivedanta Swami Prabhupāda appeared in this world in 1896 in Calcutta, India. He first met his spiritual master, Śrīla Bhaktisiddhānta Sarasvatī Gosvāmī, in Calcutta in 1922. Bhaktisiddhānta Sarasvatī, a prominent religious scholar and the founder of sixty-four Gauḍīya Maṭhas (Vedic institutes), liked this educated young man and convinced him to dedicate his life to teaching Vedic knowledge. Śrīla Prabhupāda became his student and, in 1933, his formally initiated disciple.

At their first meeting, in 1922, Śrīla Bhaktisiddhānta Sarasvatī requested Śrīla Prabhupāda to broadcast Vedic knowledge in English. In the years that followed, Śrīla Prabhupāda wrote a commentary on the *Bhagavad-gītā,* assisted the Gauḍīya Maṭha in its work, and, in 1944, started *Back to Godhead,* an English fortnightly magazine. Single-handedly, Śrīla Prabhupāda edited it, typed the manuscripts, checked the galley proofs, and even distributed the individual copies. The magazine is now being continued by his disciples in the West.

In 1950 Śrīla Prabhupāda retired from married life, adopting the *vānaprastha* (retired) order to devote more time to his studies and writing. He traveled to the holy city of Vṛndāvana, where he lived in humble circumstances in the historic temple of Rādhā-Dāmodara. There he engaged for several years in deep study and writing. He accepted the renounced order of life (*sannyāsa*) in 1959. At Rādhā-Dāmodara, Śrīla Prabhupāda began work on his life's masterpiece: a multivolume commentated translation of the eighteen-thousand-verse *Śrīmad-Bhagavatam* (*Bhāgavata Purāṇa*). He also wrote *Easy Journey to Other Planets.*

After publishing three volumes of the *Bhāgavatam,* Śrīla Prabhupāda came to the United States, in September 1965, to fulfill the mission of his spiritual master. Subsequently, His Divine Grace wrote more than fifty volumes of authoritative commentated translations and summary studies of the philosophical and religious classics of India.

When he first arrived by freighter in New York City, Śrīla Prabhupāda was practically penniless. Only after almost a year of great difficulty did he establish the International Society for Krishna Consciousness, in July of 1966. Before he passed away on November 14, 1977, he had guided the Society and seen it grow to a worldwide confederation of more than one hundred *āśramas,* schools, temples, institutes, and farm communities.

In 1972 His Divine Grace introduced the Vedic system of primary and secondary education in the West by founding the *gurukula* school in Dallas, Texas. Since then his disciples have established similar schools throughout the United States and the rest of the world.

Śrīla Prabhupāda also inspired the construction of several large international cultural centers in India. The center at Śrīdhāma Māyāpur is the site for a planned spiritual city, an ambitions project for which construction will extend over many years to come. In Vṛndāvana are the magnificent Kṛṣṇa-Balarāma Temple and International Guesthouse, *gurukula* school, and Śrīla Prabhupāda Memorial and Museum. There is also a major cultural and educational center in Bombay. Other centers are planned in a dozen important locations on the Indian subcontinent.

Śrīla Prabhupāda's most significant contribution, however, is his books. Highly respected by scholars for their authority, depth, and clarity, they are used as textbooks in numerous college courses. His writings have been translated into over fifty languages. The Bhaktivedanta Book Trust, established in 1972 to publish the works of His Divine Grace, has thus become the world's largest publisher of books in the field of Indian religion and philosophy.

In just twelve years, in spite of his advanced age, Śrīla Prabhupāda circled the globe fourteen times on lecture tours that took him to six continents. In spite of such a vigorous schedule, Śrīla Prabhupāda continued to write prolifically. His writings constitute a veritable library of Vedic philosophy, religion, literature, and culture.

Kṛṣṇa Consciousness at Home

by Mahātmā dāsa

The history of Ajāmila makes it clear how important it is for everyone to practice Kṛṣṇa consciousness, devotional service to Lord Kṛṣṇa. Of course, living in the association of Kṛṣṇa's devotees in a temple or *āśrama* makes it easier to practice devotional service. But if you're determined, you can follow at home the teachings of Kṛṣṇa consciousness and thus convert your home into a temple.

Spiritual life, like material life, means practical activity. The difference is that whereas we perform material activities for the benefit of ourselves or those we consider ours, we perform spiritual activities for the benefit of Lord Kṛṣṇa, under the guidance of the scriptures and the spiritual master. The key is to accept the guidance of the scripture and the *guru*. Kṛṣṇa declares in the *Bhagavad-gītā* that a person can achieve neither happiness nor the supreme destination of life—going back to Godhead, back to Lord Kṛṣṇa—if he or she does not follow the injunctions of the scriptures. And *how* to follow the scriptural rules by engaging in practical service to the Lord—that is explained by a bona fide spiritual master. Without following the instructions of a spiritual master who is in an authorized chain of disciplic succession coming from Kṛṣṇa Himself, we cannot make spiritual progress. The practices outlined here are the timeless practices of *bhakti-yoga* as given by the foremost spiritual master and exponent of Kṛṣṇa consciousness in our time, His Divine Grace A. C. Bhaktivedanta Swami Prabhupāda, founder-*ācārya* of the International Society for Krishna Consciousness (ISKCON).

The purpose of spiritual knowledge is to bring us closer to God, or Kṛṣṇa. Kṛṣṇa says in the *Bhagavad-gītā* (18.55), *bhaktyā mām abhijānāti:* "I can be known only by devotional service." Knowledge guides us in proper action. Spiritual knowledge directs us to satisfy the desires of Kṛṣṇa through practical engagements in His loving service. Without practical application, theoretical knowledge is of little value.

Spiritual knowledge is meant to direct us in all aspects of life. We should endeavor, therefore, to organize our lives in such a way as to follow Kṛṣṇa's teachings as far as possible. We should try to do our best, to do more than is simply convenient. Then it will be possible for us to rise to the transcendental plane of Kṛṣṇa consciousness, even while living far from a temple.

Chanting the Hare Kṛṣṇa Mantra

The first principle in devotional service is to chant the Hare Kṛṣṇa *mahā-mantra* (*mahā* means "great"; *mantra* means "sound that liberates the mind from ignorance"):

Hare Kṛṣṇa, Hare Kṛṣṇa, Kṛṣṇa Kṛṣṇa, Hare Hare
Hare Rāma, Hare Rāma, Rāma Rāma, Hare Hare

You can chant these holy names of the Lord anywhere and at any time, but it is best to set a specific time of the day to regularly chant. Early morning hours are ideal.

The chanting can be done in two ways: singing the *mantra*, called *kīrtana* (usually done in a group), and saying the *mantra* to oneself, called *japa* (which literally means "to speak softly"). Concentrate on hearing the sound of the holy names. As you chant, pronounce the names clearly and distinctly, addressing Kṛṣṇa in a prayerful mood. When your mind wanders, bring it back to the sound of the Lord's names. Chanting is a prayer to Kṛṣṇa that means "O energy of the Lord [Hare], O all-attractive Lord [Kṛṣṇa], O Supreme Enjoyer [Rāma], please engage me in Your service." The more attentively and sincerely you chant these names of God, the more spiritual progress you will make.

Since God is all-powerful and all-merciful, He has kindly made it very easy for us to chant His names, and He has also invested all His powers in them. Therefore the names of God and God Himself are identical. This means that when we chant the holy names of Kṛṣṇa and Rāma we are directly associating with God and being purified. Therefore we should always try to chant with devotion and reverence. The Vedic literature states that Lord Kṛṣṇa is personally dancing on your tongue when you chant His holy name.

When you chant alone, it is best to chant on *japa* beads (available from Temple Services, at one of the addresses given in the advertisement at the end of this book). This not only helps you fix your attention on the holy name, but it also helps you count the number of times you chant the *mantra* daily. Each strand of *japa* beads contains 108 small beads and one large bead, the head bead. Begin on a bead next to the head bead and gently roll it between the thumb and middle finger of your right hand as you chant the full Hare Kṛṣṇa *mantra*. Then move to the next bead and repeat the process. In this way, chant on each of the 108 beads until you reach the head bead again. This is one round of *japa*. Then, without chanting on the head bead, reverse the beads and start your second round on the last bead you chanted on.

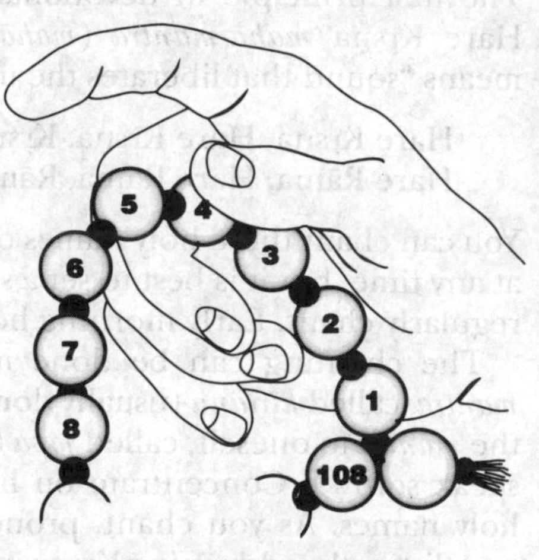

Initiated devotees vow before the spiritual master to chant at least sixteen rounds of the Hare Kṛṣṇa *mantra* daily. But even if you can chant only one round a day, the principle is that once you commit yourself to chanting that round, you should try complete it every day without fail. When you feel you can chant more, then increase the minimum number of rounds you chant each day—but don't fall below that number. You can chant more than your fixed number, but you should maintain a set minimum each day. (Please note that the beads are sacred and therefore should never touch the ground or be put in an unclean place. To keep your beads clean, it's best to carry them in a special bead bag, also available from Temple Services.)

Aside from chanting *japa,* you can also sing the Lord's holy names in *kīrtana.* While you can perform *kīrtana* individually, it is generally performed with others. A melodious *kīrtana* with family or friends is sure to enliven everyone. ISKCON devotees use traditional melodies and instruments, especially in the temple, but you can chant to any melody and use any musical instruments to accompany your chanting. As Lord Caitanya said, "There are no hard and fast rules for chanting Hare Kṛṣṇa." One thing you might want to do, however, is order some *kīrtana* and *japa* audiotapes from Temple Services.

Setting Up Your Altar

You will likely find that your *japa* and *kīrtana* are especially effective when done before an altar. Lord Kṛṣṇa and His pure devotees are so kind that they allow us to worship them even through their pictures. It is something like mailing a letter: You cannot mail a letter by placing it in just any box; you must use the mailbox authorized by the government. Similarly, we cannot imagine a picture of God and worship that, but we can worship the authorized picture of God, and Kṛṣṇa accepts our worship through that picture.

Setting up an altar at home means receiving the Lord and His pure devotees as your most honored guests. Where should you set up the altar? Well, how would you seat a guest? An ideal place would be clean, well lit, and free from drafts and household disturbances. Your guest, of course, would need a comfortable chair, but for the picture of Kṛṣṇa's form a wall shelf, a mantelpiece, a corner table, or the top shelf of a bookcase will do. You wouldn't seat a guest in your home and then ignore him; you'd provide a place for yourself to sit, too, where you could comfortably face him and enjoy his company. So don't make your altar inaccessible.

What do you need for an altar? Here are the essentials:

1. A picture of Śrīla Prabhupāda.
2. A picture of Lord Caitanya and His associates.
3. A picture of Śrī Śrī Rādhā-Kṛṣṇa.

In addition, you may want an altar cloth, water cups (one for each picture), candles with holders, a special plate for offering food, a small bell, incense, an incense holder, and fresh flowers, which you may offer in vases or simply place before each picture. If you're interested in more elaborate Deity worship, ask any of the ISKCON devotees or write to Temple Services.

The first person we worship on the altar is the spiritual master. The spiritual master is not God. Only God is God. But because the spiritual master is His dearmost servant, God has empowered him, and therefore he deserves the same respect as that given to God. He links the disciple with God and teaches him the process of *bhakti-yoga*. He is God's ambassador to the material world. When a president sends an ambassador to a foreign country, the ambassador receives the same respect as that accorded the president, and the ambassador's words are as authoritative as the president's. Similarly, we should respect the spiritual master as we would God, and revere his words as we would His.

There are two main kinds of *gurus:* the instructing *guru* and the initiating *guru*. Everyone who takes up the process of *bhakti-yoga* as a result of coming in contact with

ISKCON owes an immense debt of gratitude to Śrīla Prabhupāda. Before Śrīla Prabhupāda left India in 1965 to spread Kṛṣṇa consciousness abroad, almost no one outside India knew anything about the practice of pure devotional service to Lord Kṛṣṇa. Therefore, everyone who has learned of the process through his books, his *Back to Godhead* magazine, his tapes, or contact with his followers should offer respect to Śrīla Prabhupāda. As the founder and spiritual guide of the International Society for Krishna Consciousness, he is the instructing *guru* of us all.

As you progress in *bhakti-yoga*, you may eventually want to accept initiation. Before he left this world in 1977, Śrīla Prabhupāda authorized a system in which advanced and qualified devotees would carry on his work by initiating disciples in accordance with his instructions. At present there are many spiritual masters in ISKCON. To learn how you can get in touch with them for spiritual guidance and association, ask a devotee at your nearby temple, or write to the president of one of the ISKCON centers listed at the end of this book.

The second picture on your altar should be one of the *pañca-tattva*, Lord Caitanya and His four leading associates. Lord Caitanya is the incarnation of God for this age. He is Kṛṣṇa Himself, descended in the form of His own devotee to teach us how to surrender to Him, specifically by chanting His holy names and performing other activities of *bhakti-yoga*. Lord Caitanya is the most merciful incarnation, for He makes it easy for anyone to attain love of God through the chanting of the Hare Kṛṣṇa *mantra*.

And of course your altar should have a picture of the Supreme Personality of Godhead, Lord Śrī Kṛṣṇa, with His eternal consort, Śrīmatī Rādhārāṇī. Śrīmatī Rādhārāṇī is Kṛṣṇa's spiritual potency. She is devotional service personified, and devotees always take shelter of Her to learn how to serve Kṛṣṇa.

You can arrange the pictures in a triangle, with the picture of Śrīla Prabhupāda on the left, the picture of Lord Caitanya and His associates on the right, and the picture of

Rādhā and Kṛṣṇa, which, if possible, should be slightly larger than the others, on a small raised platform behind and in the center. Or you can hang the picture of Rādhā and Kṛṣṇa on the wall above.

Carefully clean the altar each morning. Cleanliness is essential in Deity worship. Remember, you wouldn't neglect to clean the room of an important guest, and when you establish an altar you invite Kṛṣṇa and His pure devotees to reside as the most exalted guests in your home. If you have water cups, rinse them out and fill them with fresh water daily. Then place them conveniently close to the pictures. You should remove flowers in vases as soon as they're slightly wilted, or daily if you've offered them at the base of the pictures. You should offer fresh incense at least once a day, and, if possible, light candles and place them near the pictures when you're chanting before the altar.

Please try the things we've suggested so far. It's very simple, really: If you try to love God, you'll gradually realize how much He loves you. That's the essence of *bhakti-yoga.*

Prasādam: How to Eat Spiritually

By His immense transcendental energies, Kṛṣṇa can actually convert matter into spirit. If we place an iron rod in a fire, before long the rod becomes red hot and acts just like fire. In the same way, food prepared for and offered to Kṛṣṇa with love and devotion becomes completely spiritualized. Such food is called Kṛṣṇa *prasādam,* which means "the mercy of Lord Kṛṣṇa."

Eating *prasādam* is a fundamental practice of *bhakti-yoga.* In other forms of *yoga* one must artificially repress the senses, but the *bhakti-yogī* can engage his or her senses in a variety of pleasing spiritual activities, such as tasting delicious food offered to Lord Kṛṣṇa. In this way the senses gradually become spiritualized and bring the devotee more and more transcendental pleasure by being engaged in devotional service. Such spiritual pleasure far surpasses any material experience.

Lord Caitanya said of *prasādam,* "Everyone has tasted these foods before. However, now that they have been prepared for Kṛṣṇa and offered to Him with devotion, these foods have acquired extraordinary tastes and uncommon fragrances. Just taste them and see the difference in the experience! Apart from the taste, even the fragrance pleases the mind and makes one forget any other fragrance. Therefore, it should be understood that the spiritual nectar of Kṛṣṇa's lips must have touched these ordinary foods and imparted to them all their transcendental qualities."

Eating only food offered to Kṛṣṇa is the perfection of vegetarianism. In itself, being a vegetarian is not enough; after all, even pigeons and monkeys are vegetarians. But when we go beyond vegetarianism to a diet of *prasādam,* our eating becomes helpful in achieving the goal of human life—reawakening the soul's original relationship with God. In the *Bhagavad-gītā* Lord Kṛṣṇa says that unless one eats only food that has been offered to Him in sacrifice, one will suffer the reactions of *karma.*

How to Prepare and Offer Prasādam

As you walk down the supermarket aisles selecting the foods you will offer to Kṛṣṇa, you need to know what is offerable and what is not. In the *Bhagavad-gītā,* Lord Kṛṣṇa states, "If one offers Me with love and devotion a leaf, a flower, a fruit, or water, I will accept it." From this verse it is understood that we can offer Kṛṣṇa foods prepared from milk products, vegetables, fruits, nuts, and grains. (Write to Temple Services for one of the many Hare Kṛṣṇa cookbooks.) Meat, fish, and eggs are not offerable. And a few vegetarian items are also forbidden—garlic and onions, for example, which are in the mode of darkness. (*Hing,* or asafetida, is a tasty substitute for them in cooking and is available at most Indian groceries or from Temple Services.) Nor can you offer to Kṛṣṇa coffee or tea that contain caffeine. If you like these beverages, purchase caffeine-free coffee and herbal teas.

While shopping, be aware that you may find meat, fish, and egg products mixed with other foods; so be sure to read labels carefully. For instance, some brands of yogurt and sour cream contain gelatin, a substance made from the horns, hooves, and bones of slaughtered animals. Also, make sure the cheese you buy contains no rennet, an enzyme extracted from the stomach tissues of slaughtered calves. Most hard cheese sold in America contains rennet, so be careful about any cheese you can't verify as rennetless.

Also avoid foods cooked by nondevotees. According to the subtle laws of nature, the cook acts upon the food not only physically but mentally as well. Food thus becomes an agent for subtle influences on your consciousness. The principle is the same as that at work with a painting: a painting is not simply a collection of strokes on a canvas but an expression of the artist's state of mind, which affects the viewer. So if you eat food cooked by nondevotees—employees working in a factory, for example—then you're sure to absorb a dose of materialism and *karma.* So as far as possible use only fresh, natural ingredients.

In preparing food, cleanliness is the most important principle. Nothing impure should be offered to God; so keep your kitchen very clean. Always wash your hands thoroughly before entering the kitchen. While preparing food, do not taste it, for you are cooking the meal not for yourself but for the pleasure of Kṛṣṇa. Arrange portions of the food on dinnerware kept especially for this purpose; no one but the Lord should eat from these dishes. The easiest way to offer food is simply to pray, "My dear Lord Kṛṣṇa, please accept this food," and to chant each of the following prayers three times while ringing a bell (see the Sanskrit Pronunciation Guide on page 195):

1. Prayer to Śrīla Prabhupāda:

nama oṁ viṣṇu-pādāya kṛṣṇa-preṣṭhāya bhū-tale
śrīmate bhaktivedānta-svāmin iti nāmine

namas te sārasvate deve gaura-vāṇī-pracāriṇe
nirviśeṣa-śūnyavādi-pāścātya-deśa-tāriṇe

"I offer my respectful obeisances unto His Divine Grace A. C. Bhaktivedanta Swami Prabhupāda, who is very dear to Lord Kṛṣṇa, having taken shelter at His lotus feet. Our respectful obeisances are unto you, O spiritual master, servant of Bhaktisiddhānta Sarasvatī Gosvāmī. You are kindly preaching the message of Lord Caitanyadeva and delivering the Western countries, which are filled with impersonalism and voidism."

2. Prayer to Lord Caitanya:

namo mahā-vadānyāya kṛṣṇa-prema-pradāya te
kṛṣṇāya kṛṣṇa-caitanya-nāmne gaura-tviṣe namaḥ

"O most munificent incarnation! You are Kṛṣṇa Himself appearing as Śrī Kṛṣṇa Caitanya Mahāprabhu. You have assumed the golden color of Śrīmatī Rādhārāṇī, and You are widely distributing pure love of Kṛṣṇa. We offer our respectful obeisances unto You."

3. Prayer to Lord Kṛṣṇa:

namo brahmaṇya-devāya go-brāhmaṇa-hitāya ca
jagad-dhitāya kṛṣṇāya govindāya namo namaḥ

"I offer my respectful obeisances unto Lord Kṛṣṇa, who is the worshipable Deity for all *brāhmaṇas,* the well-wisher of the cows and the *brāhmaṇas,* and the benefactor of the whole world. I offer my repeated obeisances to the Personality of Godhead, known as Kṛṣṇa and Govinda."

Remember that the real purpose of preparing and offering food to the Lord is to show your devotion and gratitude to Him. Kṛṣṇa accepts your devotion, not the physical offering itself. God is complete in Himself—He doesn't need anything—but out of His immense kindness He allows us to offer food to Him so that we can develop our love for Him.

After offering the food to the Lord, wait at least five minutes for Him to partake of the preparations. Then you should transfer the food from the special dinnerware and wash the dishes and utensils you used for the offering. Now you and any guests may eat the *prasādam*. While you eat, try to appreciate the spiritual value of the food. Remember that because Kṛṣṇa has accepted it, it is nondifferent from Him, and therefore by eating it you will become purified.

Everything you offer on your altar becomes *prasādam*, the mercy of the Lord. Flowers, incense, the water, the food—everything you offer for the Lord's pleasure becomes spiritualized. The Lord enters into the offerings, and thus the remnants are nondifferent from Him. So you should not only deeply respect the things you've offered, but you should distribute them to others as well. Distribution of *prasādam* is an essential part of Deity worship.

Everyday Life: The Four Regulative Principles

Anyone serious about progressing in Kṛṣṇa consciousness must try to avoid the following four sinful activities:

1. **Eating meat, fish, or eggs.** These foods are saturated with the modes of passion and ignorance and therefore cannot be offered to the Lord. A person who eats these foods participates in a conspiracy of violence against helpless animals and thus stops his spiritual progress dead in its tracks.

2. **Gambling.** Gambling invariably puts one into anxiety and fuels greed, envy, and anger.

3. **The use of intoxicants.** Drugs, alcohol, and tobacco, as well as any drinks or foods containing caffeine, cloud the mind, overstimulate the senses, and make it impossible to understand or follow the principles of *bhakti-yoga*.

4. **Illicit sex.** This is sex outside of marriage or sex in marriage for any purpose other than procreation. Sex for pleasure compels one to identify with the body and takes one far from Kṛṣṇa consciousness. The scriptures teach that sex is the most powerful force binding us to the material world. Anyone serious about advancing in Kṛṣṇa consciousness should minimize sex or eliminate it entirely.

Engagement in Practical Devotional Service

Everyone must do some kind of work, but if you work only for yourself you must accept the karmic reactions of that work. As Lord Kṛṣṇa says in the *Bhagavad-gītā* (3.9), "Work done as a sacrifice for Viṣṇu [Kṛṣṇa] has to be performed. Otherwise work binds one to the material world."

You needn't change your occupation, except if you're now engaged in a sinful job such as working as a butcher or bartender. If you're a writer, write for Kṛṣṇa; if you're an artist, create for Kṛṣṇa; if you're a secretary, type for Kṛṣṇa. You may also directly help the temple in your spare time, and you should sacrifice some of the fruits of your work by contributing a portion of your earnings to help maintain the temple and propagate Kṛṣṇa consciousness. Some devotees living outside the temple buy Hare Kṛṣṇa literature and distribute it to their friends and associates, or they engage in a variety of services at the temple. There is also a wide network of devotees who gather in each other's homes for chanting, worship, and study. Write to your local temple or the Society's secretary to learn of any such programs near you.

Additional Devotional Principles

There are many more devotional practices that can help you become Kṛṣṇa conscious. Here are two vital ones:

Studying Hare Kṛṣṇa literature. Śrīla Prabhupāda, the founder-*ācārya* of ISKCON, dedicated much of his time to writing books such as the *Śrīmad-Bhāgavatam,* the source of the Ajāmila story. Hearing the words—or reading the writings—of a realized spiritual master is an essential spiritual practice. So try to set aside some time every day to read Śrīla Prabhupāda's books. You can get a free catalog of available books and tapes from Temple Services.

Associating with devotees. Śrīla Prabhupāda established the Hare Kṛṣṇa movement to give people in general the chance to associate with devotees of the Lord. This is the best way to gain faith in the process of Kṛṣṇa consciousness and become enthusiastic in devotional service. Conversely, maintaining intimate connections with nondevotees slows one's spiritual progress. So try to visit the Hare Kṛṣṇa center nearest you as often as possible.

In Closing

The beauty of Kṛṣṇa consciousness is that you can take as much as you're ready for. Kṛṣṇa Himself promises in the *Bhagavad-gītā* (2.40), "There is no loss or diminution in this endeavor, and even a little advancement on this path protects one from the most fearful type of danger." So bring Kṛṣṇa into your daily life, and we guarantee you'll feel the benefit.

Hare Kṛṣṇa!

Sanskrit Pronunciation Guide

The system of transliteration used in this book conforms to a system that scholars have accepted to indicate the pronunciation of each sound in the Sanskrit language.

The short vowel **a** is pronounced like the **u** in b**u**t, long **ā** like the **a** in f**a**r. Short **i** is pronounced as in p**i**n, long **ī** as in p**i**que, short **u** as in p**u**ll, and long **ū** as in r**u**le. The vowel **ṛ** is pronounced like the **ri** in **ri**m, **e** like the **ey** in th**ey**, **o** like the **o** in g**o**, **ai** like the **ai** in **ai**sle, and **au** like the **ow** in h**ow**. The *anusvāra* (**ṁ**) is pronounced like the **n** in the French word *bo***n**, and *visarga* (**ḥ**) is pronounced as a final **h** sound. At the end of a couplet, **aḥ** is pronounced **aha**, and **iḥ** is pronounced **ihi**.

The guttural consonants—**k, kh, g, gh,** and **ṅ**—are pronounced from the throat in much the same manner as in English. **K** is pronounced as in **k**ite, **kh** as in Ec**kh**art, **g** as in **g**ive, **gh** as in di**g h**ard, and **ṅ** as in si**ng**.

The palatal consonants—**c, ch, j, jh,** and **ñ**—are pronounced with the tongue touching the firm ridge behind the teeth. **C** is pronounced as in **ch**air, **ch** as in staun**ch-h**eart, **j** as in **j**oy, **jh** as in he**dgeh**og, and **ñ** as in ca**n**yon.

The cerebral consonants—**ṭ, ṭh, ḍ, ḍh,** and **ṇ**—are pronounced with the tip of the tongue turned up and drawn back against the dome of the palate. **Ṭ** is pronounced as in **t**ub, **ṭh** as in ligh**t-h**eart, **ḍ** as in **d**ove, **ḍh** as in re**d-h**ot, and **ṇ** as in **n**ut. The dental consonants—**t, th, d, dh,** and **n**—are pronounced in the same manner as the cerebrals, but with the forepart of the tongue against the teeth.

The labial consonants—**p, ph, b, bh,** and **m**—are pronounced with the lips. **P** is pronounced as in **p**ine, **ph** as in u**ph**ill, **b** as in **b**ird, **bh** as in ru**b-h**ard, and **m** as in **m**other.

The semivowels—**y, r, l,** and **v**—are pronounced as in **y**es, **r**un, **l**ight, and **v**ine respectively. The sibilants—**ś, ṣ,** and **s**—are pronounced, respectively, as in the German word **s***prechen* and the English words **sh**ine and **s**un. The letter **h** is pronounced as in **h**ome.

Index

The International Society for Krishna Consciousness

Centers Around the World

Founder-Ācārya: His Divine Grace A. C. Bhaktivedanta Swami Prabhupāda

♦ Temples with restaurants or dining.

NORTH AMERICA

CANADA

Calgary, Alberta — 313 Fourth St. N.E., T2E 3S3/ Tel. (403) 238-0602
Montreal, Quebec — 1626 Pie IX Boulevard, H1V 2C5/ Tel. (514) 521-1301
♦ **Ottawa, Ontario** — 212 Somerset St. E., K1N 6V4/ Tel. (613) 565-6544
Regina, Saskatchewan — 1279 Retallack St., S4T 2H8/ Tel. (306) 525-1640
♦ **Toronto, Ontario** — 243 Avenue Rd., M5R 2J6/ Tel. (416) 922-5415
♦ **Vancouver, B.C.** — 5462 S.E. Marine Dr., Burnaby V5J 3G8/ Tel. (604) 433-9728
Victoria, B.C.—1505 Arrow Rd., V8N 1C3/ Tel. (604) 721-2102

FARM COMMUNITY

Ashcroft, B.C. — Saranagati Dhama, Box 99, V0K 1A0

ADDITIONAL RESTAURANTS

Hamilton, Ontario — Govinda's, 195 Locke St. South, L8T 4B5/ Tel. (416) 523-6209
Vancouver — The Hare Krishna Place, 46 Begbie St., New Westminster

U.S.A.

♦ **Atlanta, Georgia** — 1287 South Ponce de Leon Ave. N.E., 30306/ Tel. (404) 378-9234
Baltimore, Maryland — 200 Bloomsbury Ave., Catonsville, 21228/ Tel. (410) 744-1624 or 4069
Boise, Idaho — 1615 Martha St., 83706/ Tel. (208) 344-4274
Boston, Massachusetts — 72 Com-monwealth Ave., 02116/ Tel. (617) 247-8611
Champaign, Illinois — 608 W. Elm St., 61801/ Tel. (217) 344-2562
♦ **Chicago, Illinois** — 1716 W. Lunt Ave., 60626/ Tel. (312) 973-0900
Columbus, Ohio — 379 W. Eighth Ave., 43201/ Tel. (614) 421-1661
♦ **Dallas, Texas** — 5430 Gurley Ave., 75223/ Tel. (214) 827-6330
♦ **Denver, Colorado** — 1400 Cherry St., 80220/ Tel. (303) 333-5461
♦ **Detroit, Michigan** — 383 Lenox Ave., 48215/ Tel. (313) 824-6000
Encinitas,California — 468 First St., 92024/ Tel. (619) 634-1698
Gainesville, Florida — 214 N.W. 14th St., 32603/ Tel. (904) 336-4183
Gurabo, Puerto Rico — Route 181, P.O. Box 8440 HC-01, 00778-9763/ Tel. (809) 737-1658
Hartford, Connecticut — 1683 Main St., E. Hartford, 06108/ Tel. (203) 289-7252
♦ **Honolulu, Hawaii** — 51 Coelho Way, 96817/ Tel. (808) 595-3947
Houston, Texas — 1320 W. 34th St., 77018/ Tel. (713) 686-4482
♦ **Laguna Beach, California** — 285 Legion St., 92651/ Tel. (714) 494-7029
Long Island, New York — 197 S. Ocean Ave., Freeport, 11520/ Tel. (516) 867-9045
♦ **Los Angeles, California** — 3764 Watseka Ave., 90034/ Tel. (310) 836-2676
♦ **Miami, Florida** — 3220 Virginia St., 33133 (mail: P.O. Box 337, Coconut Grove, FL 33233)/ Tel. (305) 442-7218
♦ **New Orleans, Louisiana** — 2936 Esplanade Ave., 70119/ Tel. (504) 586-9379
New York, New York — 305 Schermerhorn St., Brooklyn, 11217/ Tel. (718) 855-6714
New York, New York — 26 Second Avenue, 10003/ Tel. (212) 420-8803
Philadelphia, Pennsylvania — 41 West Allens Lane, 19119/ Tel. (215) 247-4600
Portland, Oregon — 5137 N.E. 42 Ave., 97218/ Tel. (503) 234-8971
♦ **St. Louis, Missouri** — 3926 Lindell Blvd., 63108/ Tel. (314) 535-8085
San Diego, California — 1030 Grand Ave., Pacific Beach, 92109/ Tel. (619) 483-2500
San Francisco, California — 84 Carl St., 94117/ Tel. (415) 661-7320
♦ **San Francisco, California** — 2334 Stuart St., Berkeley, 94705/Tel. (510) 540-9215
Seattle, Washington — 1420 228th Ave. S.E., Issaquah, 98027/ Tel. (206) 391-3293
Spanish Fork, Utah — KHQN Radio, 8628 South State St., 84660/ Tel. (801) 798-3559
Tallahassee, Florida — 1323 Nylic St. (mail: P.O. Box 20224, 32304)/ Tel. (904) 681-9258
Topanga, California — 20395 Callon Dr., 90290/ Tel. (213) 455-1658
Towaco, New Jersey — P.O. Box 109, 07082/ Tel. (201) 299-0970
♦ **Tucson, Arizona** — 711 E. Blacklidge Dr., 85719/ Tel. (602) 792-0630
Walla Walla, Washington — 314 E. Poplar, 99362/ Tel. (509) 525-7133
Washington, D.C. — 600 Ninth St, NE, 20002/ Tel. (202) 547-1444
Washington, D.C. — 10310 Oaklyn Dr., Potomac, Maryland 20854/ Tel. (301) 299-2100

FARM COMMUNITIES

Alachua, Florida (New Ramana-reti) — Box 819, 32615/ Tel. (904) 462-2017
Carriere, Mississippi (New Talavan) — 31492 Anner Road, 39426/ Tel. (601) 799-1354
Gurabo, Puerto Rico (New Govardhana Hill) — (contact ISKCON Gurabo)
Hillsborough, North Carolina (New Goloka) — 1032 Dimmocks Mill Rd., 27278/ Tel. (919) 732-6492
Mulberry, Tennessee (Murari-sevaka) — Rt. No. 1, Box 146-A, 37359/ Tel (615) 759-6888
Port Royal, Pennsylvania (Gita Nagari) — R.D. No. 1, Box 839, 17082/ Tel. (717) 527-4101

ADDITIONAL RESTAURANTS AND DINING

Boise, Idaho — Govinda's, 500 W. Main St., 83702/ Tel. (208) 338-9710
Eugene, Oregon — Govinda's Vegetarian Buffet, 270 W. 8th St., 97401/ Tel. (503) 686-3531
Gainesville, Florida — Radha's, 125 NW 23rd Ave., 32609/ Tel. (904) 376-9012
Gurabo, Puerto Rico — 1 (809) 737-7039

EUROPE

UNITED KINGDOM AND IRELAND

Belfast, Northern Ireland — 140 Upper Dunmurray

Lane, BT17 OHE/ Tel. +44 (01232) 620530
Birmingham, England — 84 Stanmore Rd., Edgebaston, B16 9TB/ Tel. +44 (0121) 420-4999
Bristol, England — 48 Station Rd., Nailsea, Bristol BS19 2PB/ Tel. +44 (01275) 853788
Coventry, England — Sri Sri Radha Krishna Cultural Centre, Kingfield Rd., Radford (mail: 19 Gloucester St., CV1 3BZ)/ Tel. +44 (01203) 555420
Dublin, Ireland — 56 Dame St., Dublin 2/ Tel. +353 (01) 679-1306
Glasgow, Scotland — Karuna Bhavan, Bankhouse Rd., Lesmahagow, Lanarkshire ML11 0ES/ Tel. +44 (01555) 894790
Leicester, England — 21/21A Thoresby St., North Evington, Leicester LE5 4GU/ Tel. +44 (01533) 762587
Liverpool, England — 114A Bold St., Liverpool L1 4HY/ Tel. +44 (0151) 708 9400
♦ **London, England (city)** — 10 Soho St., London W1V 5DA/ Tel. +44 (0171) 4373662 (business hours), 4393606 (other times); Govinda's Restaurant: 4374928
London, England (country) — Bhaktivedanta Manor, Letchmore Heath, Watford, Hertfordshire WD2 8EP/ Tel. +44 (01923) 857244
London, England (south) — 42 Enmore Road, South Norwood, London SE25/ Tel. +44 (0181) 656-4296
Manchester, England — 20 Mayfield Rd., Whalley Range, Manchester M16 8FT/ Tel. +44 (0161) 2264416
Newcastle upon Tyne, England — 21 Leazes Park Rd., NE1 4PF/ Tel. +44 (0191) 2220150

GERMANY

♦ **Berlin** — Bhakti Yoga Center, Muskauer Str. 27, 10997 Berlin/ Tel. +49 (030) 618 9112
Flensburg — Neuhoerup 1, 24980 Hoerup/ Tel. +49 (04639) 73 36
Hamburg — Muehlenstr. 93, 25421 Pinneberg/ Tel. +49 (04101) 2 39 31
♦ **Heidelberg** — Center for Vedic Studies, Kürfuersten-Anlage 5, 69115 Heidelberg (mail: P.O. Box 101726, 69007 Heidelberg)/ Tel. +49 (06221) 16 51 01
♦ **Köln** — Taunusstr. 40, 51105 Köln/ Tel. +49 (0221) 830 37 78
Munich — Tal 38, 80331 Munchen/ Tel +49 (089) 29 23 17
Nuremberg — Bhakti Yoga Center, Kopernikusplatz 12, 90459 Nürnberg/ Tel. +49 (0911) 45 32 86
Weimar — Rothauserbergweg 6, 99425 Weimar/ Tel. +49 (03643) 5 95 48
Wiesbaden — Schiersteiner Strasse 6, 65187 Wiesbaden/ Tel. +49 (0611) 37 33 12

ITALY

Asti — Roatto, Frazione Valle Reale 20/ Tel. +39 (0141) 938406
Bergamo — Villaggio Hare Krishna, Via Galileo Galilei 41, 24040 Chignolo D'isola (BG)/ Tel. +39 (035) 490706
Bologna — Via Ramo Barchetta 2, 40010 Bentivoglio (BO)/ Tel. +39 (051) 863924
♦ **Catania** — Via San Nicolo al Borgo 28, 95128 Catania, Sicily/ jTel. +39 (095) 522-252
Naples — Via Vesuvio, N33, Ercolano LNA7/ Tel. +39 (081) 739-0398
Rome — Nepi, Sri Gaura Mandala, Via Mazzanese Km. 0,700 (dalla Cassia uscita Calcata), Pian del Pavone (Viterbo)/ Tel. +39 (0761) 527038
Vicenza — Via Roma 9, 36020 Albettone (Vicenza)/ Tel. +39 (0444) 790573 or 790566

SWEDEN

Göthenburg — Hojdgatan 22, 431 36 Moelndal/ Tel. +46 (031) 879648
♦ **Grödinge** — Korsnäs Gård, 14792 Grödinge/ Tel. +46 (8530) 29151
Karlstad — ISKCON, Box 5155, 650 05 Karlstadø
♦ **Lund** — Bredg 28 ipg, 222 21/ Tel. +46 (046) 120413
Malmö — Hare Krishna Temple, Gustav Adolfs Torg 10 A, 211 39 Malmö/ Tel. +46 (040) 127181
♦ **Stockholm** — Fridhemsgatan 22, 11240 Stockholm/ Tel. +46 (08) 6549 002
♦ **Uppsala** — Nannaskolan sal F.3, Kungsgatan 22 (mail: Box 833, 751 08, Uppsala)/ Tel. +46 (018) 102924 or 509956

SWITZERLAND

Basel — Hammerstrasse 11, 4058 Basel/ Tel. +41 (061) 693 26 38
Bern — Marktgasse 7, 3011 Bern/ Tel. +41 (031) 312 38 25
Lugano — Via ai Grotti, 6862 Rancate (TI)/ Tel. +41 (091) 46 66 16
Zürich — Bergstrasse 54, 8030 Zürich/ Tel. +41 (1) 262-33-88
♦ **Zürich** — Preyergrasse 16, 8001 Zürich/ Tel. +41 (1) 251-88-51

OTHER COUNTRIES

Amsterdam, The Netherlands — Van Hilligaertstraat 17, 1072 JX, Amsterdam/ Tel. +31 (020) 6751404
Antwerp, Belgium — Amerikalei 184, 2000 Antwerpen/ Tel. +32 (03) 237-0037
Athens, Greece — Methymnis 18, Kipseli, 11257 Athens/ Tel. +30 (01) 8658384
Barcelona, Spain — c/de L'Oblit 67, 08026 Barcelona/ Tel. +34 (93) 347-9933
Belgrade, Serbia — VVZ-Veda, Custendilska 17, 11000 Beograd/ Tel. +381 (11) 781-695
Budapest, Hungary — Hare Krishna Temple, Mariaremetei ut. 77, Budapest 1028 II/Tel. +36 (01) 1768774
Copenhagen, Denmark — Baunevej 23, 3400 Hillerød/ Tel. +45 42286446
Debrecen, Hungary — L. Hegyi Mihalyne, U62, Debrecen 4030/ Tel. +36 (052) 342-496
Iasi, Romania — Stradela Moara De Vint 72, 6600 Iasi
Kaunas, Lithuania — Savanoryu 37, Kaunas/ Tel. +370 (07) 222574
Lisbon, Portugal — Rua Fernao Lopes, 6, Cascais 2750 (mail: Apartado 2489, Lisbo 1112)/ Tel. +351 (011) 286 713
Madrid, Spain — Espíritu Santo 19, 28004 Madrid/ Tel. +34 (91) 521-3096
Málaga, Spain — Ctra. Alora, 3 int., 29140 Churriana/ Tel. +34 (952) 621038
Oslo, Norway — Senter for Krishnabevissthet, Skolestien 11, 0373 Oslo 3/ Tel. +47 (022) 494790
Paris, France — 31 Rue Jean Vacquier, 93160 Noisy le Grand/ Tel. +33 (01) 43043263
Porto, Portugal — Rua S. Miguel, 19 C.P. 4000 (mail: Apartado 4108, 4002 Porto Codex)/ Tel. +351 (02) 2005469
Prague, Czech Republic — Jilova 290, Prague 5-Zlicin 155 21/ Tel. +42 (02) 3021282 or 3021608
Rotterdam, The Netherlands — Braamberg 45, 2905 BK Capelle a/d Yssel./ Tel. +31 (010) 4580873
Santa Cruz de Tenerife, Spain — C/ Castillo, 44, 4°, Santa Cruz 38003,Tenerife/ Tel. +34 (922) 241035
Sarajevo, Bosnia-Herzegovina — Saburina 11, 71000 Sarajevo/ Tel. +381 (071) 531-154
♦ **Septon-Durbuy, Belgium** — Chateau de Petite Somme, 6940 Septon-Durbuy/ Tel. +32 (086) 322926
Shyauliai, Lithuania — Vytauto 65a, 5408 Shyauliai/ Tel. +370 (014) 99323
♦ **Vienna, Austria** — Center for Vedic Studies, Rosenackerstrasse 26, 1170 Vienna/ Tel. +43 (01) 222455830

ASIA

INDIA

Ahmedabad, Gujarat — Sattelite Rd., Gandhinagar Highway Crossing, Ahmedabad 380054/ Tel. (079) 649945 or 649982
Allahabad, U. P. — 403 Baghambari Housing Scheme, Bharadwaj Puram, Allahapur, Allahabad 211006/ Tel. (0532) 609213 or 607885
Bamanbore, Gujarat — N.H. 8A, Surendra-nagar District
Bangalore, Karnataka — Hare Krishna Hill, 1 'R' Block, Chord Road, Rajaji Nagar 560010/ Tel. (080) 321956 or 342818 or 322346
♦ **Bhubaneswar, Orissa** — National Highway No. 5, Nayapali, 751001/ Tel. (0674) 413517 or 413475
♦ **Bombay, Maharashtra** — Hare Krishna Land, Juhu 400 049/ Tel. (022) 6206860
Bombay, Maharashtra — 7 K. M. Munshi Marg, Chowpatty, 400007/ Tel. (022) 3634078
Calcutta, W. Bengal — 3C Albert Rd., 700017/ Tel. (033) 2473757 or 2476075
Hyderabad, A.P. — Hare Krishna Land, Nampally Station Rd., 500001/ Tel. (040) 592018 or 552924
Imphal, Manipur — Hare Krishna Land, Airport Road, 795001/ Tel. (0385) 21587
Kurukshetra, Haryana — 369 Gudri Muhalla, Main Bazaar, 132118/ Tel. (1744) 32806 or 33529
Madras, Tamil Nadu — 59, Burkit Rd., T. Nagar, 600017/ Tel. 443266
Mangalore, Karnataka — New Bungalow, D. No. 22-3-524, near Morgans Gate, Jeppu, Mangalore (mail: P.O. Box 15, Mangalore 575001)/ Tel. (824) 28895
♦ **Mayapur, W. Bengal** — Shree Mayapur Chandrodaya Mandir, Shree Mayapur Dham, Dist. Nadia (mail: P.O. Box 10279, Ballyganj, Calcutta 700019)/ Tel. (03472) 45250
Nagpur, Maharashtra — 70 Hill Road, Ramnagar, 440010/ Tel. (0712) 529932
New Delhi — Sant Nagar Main Road (Garhi), behind Nehru Place Complex (mail: P. O. Box 7061), 110065/ Tel. (011) 6419701 or 6412058
New Delhi — 14/63, Punjabi Bagh, 110026/ Tel. (011) 5410782
Pandharpur, Maharashtra — Hare Krsna Ashram (across Chandrabhaga River), Dist. Sholapur, 413304/ Tel. (0218) 623473
Pune, Maharashtra — 4 Tarapoor Rd., Camp, 411001/ Tel. (0212) 667259
Puri, Orissa — Sipasurubull Puri, Dist. Puri
Puri, Orissa — Bhakti Kuthi, Swargadwar, Puri/ Tel. (06752) 23740
Surat, Gujarat — Rander Rd., Jahangirpura, 395005/ Tel. (0261) 685516 or 685891
Tirupati, A. P. — K.T. Road, Vinayaka Nagar, 517507/ Tel. (08574) 20114
Trivandrum, Kerala — T.C. 224/1485, WC Hospital Rd., Thycaud, 695014/ Tel. (0471) 68197
Udhampur, Jammu and Kashmir — Srila Prabhupada Ashram, Prabhupada Marg, Prabhupada Nagar, Udhampur 182101/ Tel. (0199) 298
♦ **Vrindavana, U. P.** — Krishna-Balaram Mandir, Bhaktivedanta Swami Marg, Raman Reti, Mathura Dist., 281124/ Tel. (0565) 442-478 or 442-355

OTHER COUNTRIES

Bali, Indonesia — (Contact ISKCON Jakarta)
Bangkok, Thailand — 139 Soi Puttha Osotha, New Road (near GPO), Bangkok 10500/ Tel. +66 (02) 234-1006
Cagayan de Oro, Philippines — 30 Dahlia St., Ilaya Carmen, 900 (c/o Sepulveda's Compound)
Chittagong, Bangladesh — Caitanya Cultural Society, Sri Pundarik Dham, Mekhala, Hathzari (mail: GPO Box 877, Chittagong)/ Tel. +88 (031) 225822
Colombo, Sri Lanka — 188 New Chetty St., Colombo 13/ Tel. +94 (01) 433325
Dhaka, Bangladesh — 5 Chandra Mohon Basak St., Banagram, Dhaka 1203/ Tel. +880 (02) 252428
♦ **Hong Kong** — 27 Chatam Road South, 6/F, Kowloon/ Tel. +852 7396818
Iloilo City, Philippines — 13-1-1 Tereos St., La Paz, Iloilo City, Iloilo/ Tel. +63 (033) 73391
Jakarta, Indonesia — P.O. Box 2694, Jakarta Pusat 10001/ Tel. +62 (021) 4899646
Jessore, Bangladesh — Nitai Gaur Mandir, Kathakhali Bazaar, P. O. Panjia, Dist. Jessore
Jessore, Bangladesh — Rupa-Sanatana Smriti Tirtha, Ramsara, P. O. Magura Hat, Dist. Jessore
Kathmandu, Nepal — Budhanilkantha, Kathmandu (mail: P. O. Box 3520)/ Tel. +977 (01) 225087
Kuala Lumpur, Malaysia — Lot 9901, Jalan Awan Jawa, Taman Yarl, off 5½ Mile, Jalan Kelang Lama, Petaling/ Tel. +60 (03) 780-7355, -7360, or -7369
Manila, Philippines — 170 R. Fernandez, San Juan, Metro Manila/ Tel. +63 (02) 707410
Singapore — Govinda's Gifts, 763 Mountbatten Road, Singapore 1543/ Tel. +65 440-9092
Taipei, Taiwan — (mail: c/o ISKCON Hong Kong)
Tel Aviv, Israel — P. O. Box 48163, Tel Aviv 61480/ Tel. +972 (03) 5223718
Tokyo, Japan — 1-29-2-202 Izumi, Suginami-ku, Tokyo 168/ Tel. +81 (03) 3327-1541
Yogyakarta, Indonesia — P.O. Box 25, Babarsari YK, DIY

FARM COMMUNITIES

Indonesia — Govinda Kunja (contact ISKCON Jakarta)
Malaysia — Jalan Sungai Manik, 36000 Teluk Intan, Perak
Philippines (Hare Krishna Paradise) — 231 Pagsabungan Rd., Basak, Mandaue City/ Tel. +63 (032) 83254

ADDITIONAL RESTAURANTS

Cebu, Philippines — Govinda's, 26 Sanchiangko St.
Kuala Lumpur, Malaysia — Govinda's, 16-1 Jalan Bunus Enam, Masjid India/ Tel. +60 (03) 7807355 or 7807360 or 7807369
Singapore — Govinda's Restaurant, B1-19 Cuppage Plaza 5, Koek Rd., 0922/ Tel. +65 735-6755

NOTE: This is not a complete listing.

Far from a Center?
Contact us on the Internet.

http://www.harekrishna.com/~ara/
E-mail: letters@iskcon.com

These Introductory Items Marked Down 25%

Posters

Superb Florentino linen embossed prints. All posters are 18 x 24. (Besides the three shown, there are ten others to choose from. Call for our *free* catalog.)

US$3.75 each #POS

Śrī Viṣṇu

Pārtha Sārathi

Śrīla Prabhupāda

Mantra Meditation Kit

Includes a string of 108 hand-carved *japa* beads, a cotton carrying bag, counter beads, and instructions.

US$5.00 #MMK

The Rādhā-Kṛṣṇa Temple Album

The original Apple LP produced by George Harrison, featuring "Hare Kṛṣṇa Mantra" and the "Govinda" prayers that are played daily in ISKCON temples around the world. On stereo cassette or CD.

US$3.75 for cassette #CC-6
US$11.25 for CD #CD-6

Śrīla Prabhupāda Chanting Japa

This recording of His Divine Grace A.C. Bhaktivedanta Swami Prabhupāda chanting *japa* is a favorite among young and old devotees alike.

US$2.95 for cassette #JT-1

Incense

Twenty sticks per pack, hand rolled in India. Highest quality, packed in foil.

US$1.10 per pack #INC

ORDER TOLL FREE 1-800-927-4152